The American Utopian Adventure

THE BISHOP HILL COLONY

THE AMERICAN UTOPIAN ADVENTURE

sources for the study of communitarian socialism in the United States 1680–1880

Series One

Edward D. Andrews THE COMMUNITY INDUSTRIES OF THE SHAKERS (1932)

Adin Ballou HISTORY OF THE HOPEDALE COMMUNITY from its inception to its virtual submergence in the Hopedale Parish. Edited by W. S. Heywood (1897)

Paul Brown TWELVE MONTHS IN NEW HARMONY presenting a faithful account of the principal occurrences that have taken place there during that period; interspersed with remarks (1827)

John S. Duss THE HARMONISTS. A personal history (1943)

Frederick W. Evans AUTOBIOGRAPHY OF A SHAKER and revelation of the Apocalypse. With an appendix. Enlarged edition (1888)

Parke Godwin A POPULAR VIEW OF THE DOCTRINES OF CHARLES FOURIER (1844) DEMOCRACY, CONSTRUCTIVE AND PACIFIC (1844)

Walter C. Klein JOHANN CONRAD BEISSEL, MYSTIC AND MARTINET, 1690–1768 (1942)

William J. McNiff HEAVEN ON EARTH: A PLANNED MORMON SOCIETY (1940) With "Communism among the Mormons," by Hamilton Gardner

Michael A. Mikkelsen THE BISHOP HILL COLONY. A religious, communistic settlement in Henry County, Illinois (1892) With "Eric Janson and the Bishop Hill Colony," by Silvert Erdahl

Oneida Community BIBLE COMMUNISM. A compilation from the annual reports and other publications of the Oneida Association and its branches, presenting, in connection with their history, a summary view of their religious and social theories (1853)

Marianne (Dwight) Orvis LETTERS FROM BROOK FARM 1841–1847. Edited by Amy L. Reed (1928)

Robert A. Parker A YANKEE SAINT. John Humphrey Noyes and the Oneida Community (1935)

A. J. G. Perkins & Thersa Wolfson FRANCES WRIGHT: FREE ENQUIRER. The study of a temperament (1939)

Jules Prudhommeaux ICARIE ET SON FONDATEUR, ÉTIENNE CABET. Contribution à l'étude du socialisme expérimental (1907)

Albert Shaw ICARIA. A chapter in the history of communism (1884)

I

THE BISHOP HILL COLONY

A RELIGIOUS COMMUNISTIC SETTLEMENT IN HENRY COUNTY, ILLINOIS

BY MICHAEL A. MIKKELSEN, A. M.
Fellow in History, Johns Hopkins University

with
ERIC JANSON AND THE BISHOP HILL COLONY
by
Sivert Erdahl

PORCUPINE PRESS INC.
Philadelphia 1972

Library of Congress Cataloging in Publication Data

Mikkelsen, Michael Andrew.
The Bishop Hill colony.

(The American utopian adventure)
Original ed. issued as ser. 10, no. 1 of Johns Hopkins University studies in historical and political science.
1. Bishop Hill, Ill. 2. Jansonists.
I. Title. II. Series: Johns Hopkins University. Studies in historical and political science, ser. 10, no. 1.
F549.B6M6 1972 335'.9'77338 72-187466
ISBN 0-87991-014-3

Reprinted 1972 by Porcupine Press, Inc., 1317 Filbert St., Philadelphia, Pa. 19107

Manufactured in the United States of America

PREFACE.

The author does not find it necessary to make any apology for the appearance of this little contribution to the history of the Scandinavian settlements in the Northwest. The Bishop Hill Colony will always occupy a prominent place in any history of the State of Illinois. It was founded when Chicago was but an overgrown village, and when there was not a single city worthy of the name in the State. It brought 1100 able-bodied immigrants into the county of Henry when the entire population of the county was only four times that number. It put large quantities of ready money into circulation at a time when business was largely conducted by barter and when the principal medium of exchange was the skins of fur-bearing animals. It inaugurated that mighty tide of Swedish immigration which has flooded the State of Illinois and the entire Northwest with prosperous Swedish homesteads and flourishing villages. The Bishop Hill Colony built mills, erected manufactories, and put thousands of acres of virgin soil under cultivation. It engaged in banking, and its history connects itself with that of early railroading in the State. In the days of its greatest prosperity it was the principal commercial and industrial center in all the distance between the cities of Peoria and Rock Island. Yet, in spite of its importance for the early industries of the State, the Bishop Hill Colony was primarily a religious society. The history of the Jansonists before their emigration belongs to the ecclesiastical history of Sweden. What they sought in the New World was not wealth, but freedom to worship God after their own manner. They held views that were repugnant to the Church of Sweden. It was the realization of these views which they sought in the New World. Of the character of these views, as well as of the result of the experiment, the reader of this historical sketch will be able to judge for himself.

The Bishop Hill Colony was incidentally an experiment in practical communism. Perhaps also this side of its history may not be void of interest or profit in our day, when social improvement is sought largely along similar lines. It is now, indeed, thirty years since the society was dissolved, and circumstances have been modified by the advance of civilization and the progress of the industrial revolution. But human nature is substantially the same to-day as in the day of our fathers and grandfathers, and many of the difficulties which the Jansonists encountered must be met again in any attempt to apply the theories of modern socialism to practical life.

The author has attempted to give an impartial presentation of the important facts in the history of Jansonism. These facts have not been easy of access. No complete history of the Jansonists has been written, and a large part of their documents has been either accidentally or purposely destroyed. Hence, much of the information contained in this volume has needs been gathered from the lips of surviving members of the Bishop Hill Colony. In many instances the reports were of a conflicting nature, for the Jansonists are now split up into several religious parties, and each has its separate views to uphold. But care has been taken not to accept any statement unless supported by proper collateral evidence.

Another serious obstacle encountered was the unwillingness of the Jansonists to reveal any of the "absurdities" of their religion. The author stayed several weeks among them before he was able to discover the real historic meaning of Jansonism; and Charles Nordhoff, who devotes a few pages to them in his Communistic Societies of the United States, is reported to have said, on leaving Bishop Hill, "D—— these people; I can't get anything out of them." The fact of it is that the Jansonists have outgrown their creed, and many of them are now ashamed of the views for which they were once willing to sacrifice their all. Furthermore, they have been so frequently maligned and reviled that they can hardly be blamed for having grown suspicious of the motives of strangers.

In view of this, the author's thanks are due in a special sense to Mr. Jonas Olson, now in his eighty-eighth year, but remarkably well preserved, for the liberality with which he drew upon his memory for the facts connected with the inner history of the Jansonists. Jonas Olson stood near to the person of the founder of Jansonism, and, after the great leader's death, succeeded to his authority. It is not too much to say, therefore, that without Mr. Olson's invaluable assistance this monograph could not have been written. Recognition is due also to Mrs. S. J. Anderson, Messrs. John P. Chaiser, J. W. Olson, and others for valuable assistance. The author further acknowledges his indebtedness to Messrs. John Helsen and Andreas Berglund for the use of manuscripts and original documents relating to the history of the Jansonists. Mr. Berglund's collection of original documents contained a part of the correspondence and the incompleted autobiography of Eric Janson. Mr. Helsen's manuscript notes were especially valuable. Their author is not a literary man and his collection was not intended for publication. But for many years past, in the leisure of his retirement from active life, Mr. Helsen has been perfecting his notes for the use of "some future historian."

Through the kindness of an anonymous friend the author has also had access to a certified copy of the complete transactions of the Bishop Hill Colony, the original records being no longer in existence. Mention is made elsewhere of the printed books and documents which have any bearing on the history of the Jansonists.

It might appear strange that, in spite of its scientific and general interest, no adequate attempt has been made to present a complete history of Jansonism. But it must be remembered that the Jansonists were illiterate people, who, even if they had desired to publish a history of themselves, were unequal to the task of writing one. Furthermore, the War of the Rebellion, which broke out at the time of the dissolution of the society, and other important events which followed in its wake, engrossed public attention to the exclusion of all other matters of less general importance. Still, the memory of the Bishop Hill Colony cannot die, for it is part of the pioneer history of a great and flourishing State, and is cherished in the hearts of the descendants of the Jansonists, who are to be found scattered throughout the length and the breadth of the United States.

CONTENTS.

BIBLIOGRAPHY.

Eric–Jansismen i Helsingland. Anonymous. Gefle, 1845.

Några Sangar samt Böner. Forfattade af Eric Jansson. Söderhamn, 1846. Revised ed. Galva, 1857.

Forklaring öfwer den Heliga Skrift, eller Cateches. Af Eric Jansson. Söderhamn, 1846.

Bill of Complaint in the Bishop Hill Colony Case.

Answer of the Defendants to the Bill of Complaint.

The Communistic Societies of the United States. By Charles Nordhoff. New York, 1875. Pp. 143–9.

History of Henry County. Published by H. F. Kett & Co., Chicago, 1877. Chapter on the Bishop Hill Colony.

Svenskarne i Illinois. By Eric Johnson and C. F. Peterson. Chicago, 1880. Pp. 21–54. [Mr. Johnson is a son of the founder of the Bishop Hill Colony. The interesting chapter on Bishop Hill has been compiled by him.]

Handbok i Svenska Kyrkans Historia. C. A. Cornelius. Upsala, 1875. Pp. 261–5.

De Svenska Lutherska Församlingernas Historia i Amerika. By E. Norelius. Rock Island, 1891. Pp. 61–84, containing reprint of Dr. Harald Wieselgren's article on E. Janson in Biografiskt Lexikon.

THE BISHOP HILL COLONY.

I.—Devotionalism in Helsingland from 1825 to 1842.

The history of devotionalism in Helsingland from 1825 to 1842 revolves around the person of one man. Jonas Olson was born December 18, 1802, in Söderala Parish, in the province of Helsingland. The environments of his boyhood were not of a character to encourage the development of a religious disposition. His father, Olof Olson, a coarse and illiterate peasant, was an habitual drunkard, who when in his cups was in the habit of brutally maltreating wife and children. Nor was his mother a Monica to lead him to Christ, although she loved her son after a fashion, and encouraged him in his endeavors to obtain an education. For Jonas was a bright lad, and was not satisfied with knowing how to read the hymn-book and the catechism, but aspired to learning how to write and cipher, uncommon accomplishments among the peasantry at that time. It was in these unlawful aspirations that his mother encouraged her son, by procuring the necessary writing materials, which as soon as they were discovered by the angry father were ruthlessly destroyed, with the remark that such things were not intended for peasants' sons. At the age of fifteen, when he had been confirmed in the faith of the Established Lutheran Church, Jonas was compelled to shift for himself. For five years he served an uncle on the father's side as a farm-laborer. It was here, among the peasant-fishermen on the banks of the river Ljusne, near the Gulf of Bothnia, that he learned the art of preparing salmon for the market in Stockholm. For two years he served an elder sister, and then, at the age of twenty-two, returned home to take charge of his father's estate, for the eldest son—there were three sons and two daughters—had, like his father, become incapacitated for work by strong drink. He found everything in a deplorable condition, but with the vigor of youth he set to work to repair the buildings and reclaim the waste land. In the summer-time, while employing common laborers to attend to the work in the fields, he himself bought large quantities of salmon, which he cured and disposed of to good advantage on the market in Stockholm; so that ere many years had passed it was rumored that Jonas Olson was one of the most prosperous men in the parish. The year 1825 was the epoch-making period of his life. If there was any one vice which the peasantry was addicted to more than another it was the vice of intemperance. But hand-in-hand with intemperance went general laxity of morals. The clergy was no better than the peasantry. The Rev. Mr. Sherdin never waived his privilege of dancing the first round with the bride at weddings, and drank as deep as any of his parishioners. The tithes of grain which the good pastor received he sold again to his flock in the form of distilled liquor. Moreover, it was known that at least one unfortunate girl had owned the associate pastor to be the father of her child. It was at a dance in the winter of 1825 that liquor was passed around in sacrilegious mockery of the Lord's Supper. The incident made a deep impression on Jonas Olson's mind. He became converted, and forthwith resolved to lead a new life. He renounced all worldly amusements and gave himself up to the quiet introspective life of a follower of Christ. He studied the Word of God assiduously, and read the devotional literature of the Lutheran Church, especially the works of Luther, Arndt, and Nohrborg. On his frequent visits to Stockholm he bought books and visited the public libraries, so that, for a peasant, he became an unusually well-read man. It was in Stockholm that he made the acquaintance of C. O. Rosenius, the celebrated Swedish representative of Hallean pietism, and became a constant reader of the church paper edited by him. It was here, too, that he met George Scott, an English Methodist clergyman, who was established in the Swedish capital as chaplain to Samuel Owen, a wealthy English manufacturer. Scott was a man of ability and enthusiasm, and his influence was not limited to the employes of Samuel Owen. He preached in Stockholm from 1830 to 1842 with great success, and although he had had a predecessor in a certain Methodist clergyman by the name of Stewens, he may properly be considered as the founder of the Methodist Church in Sweden. In him Jonas Olson found a warm and sympathetic friend, with whom he had many extended conversations upon religious subjects. Jonas Olson, indeed, never openly embraced Methodism, but was greatly influenced by its teachings, and even accepted its cardinal doctrine of sanctification.

It was, however, especially in the matter of temperance reform that the two friends met on common ground. Under Scott's direction Jonas Olson began to organize temperance societies in his own and neighboring parishes. At first he met with considerable opposition. The clergy objected that Jesus at Canaan had not disdained to encourage the social practice of putting the wedding guests under the table. Jonas Olson's own pastor accused him of heinous designs upon his distillery. But the Crown soon lent its support to the movement, and then the clergy were everywhere among the first to sign the pledge.

But it was not only as an organizer of temperance societies that Jonas Olson found expression for his change of attitude towards religion. Immediately upon his conversion in 1825 he had begun to preach in the conventicles of the Devotionalists, who were just then beginning to appear in Söderala Parish, in the province of Helsingland. In 1826 he married his first wife. The marriage proved a happy one, although but of short duration. The death of his wife, after only a year and a half of married life, caused him to throw himself with additional zeal into church work, and it was due to him that Devotionalism was carried to every quarter of the province of Helsingland.

The Devotionalists were pietists, using the word in the broader sense in which it is employed by Heppe and Ritschl. They did not form a separate sect. They were merely individuals who were dissatisfied with the absence of vital piety in the Established Church, and who wished to introduce a living Christianity by private preaching and by the superior piety of their lives. They were called Devotionalists, or Readers (*Läsare*), because they assembled in private houses to hold devotional meetings, and because they read their Bibles and books of devotion assiduously in their homes.

C. A. Cornelius says in his history of the Swedish Church, "If we consider European Christianity in its entirety, church work in the nineteenth century . . . has been characterized by an endeavor to repair the injury wrought by the century of the Illumination, and, if possible, to restore the old order of things."[1] It was this reactionary tendency which, in the Swedish Church, was represented by Devotionalism.

Devotionalism had this in common with other pietistic movements in the latter part of the eighteenth and the beginning of the nineteenth centuries, that it sought to purify the Church from within; that it supplemented the regular church service by conventicle worship; that it paid less attention to objective purity of doctrine than subjective piety; that, in its zeal for the simplicity and vital Christianity of the Apostolic Church, it condemned many forms of amusement and recreation in themselves entirely innocent.

The clergy in the Swedish Church not being so thoroughly and generally rationalized as in other Protestant countries, the conditions were not present for a popular religious oppo-

---

[1] C. A. Cornelius. Svenska Kyrkans Historia. Upsala, 1875, 2d ed., pp. 251-2.

sition movement of national dimensions, and thus we find that Swedish pietism did not produce any great national leader after whom it might be named. It began to spread under local leaders in the latter part of the eighteenth century. Its stronghold was Norrland, one of the great political divisions of Sweden, of which Helsingland is a subdivision.

Economically, the province of Helsingland is well situated. It possesses rich iron mines, which yield a large annual produce. It also possesses linen and other manufactures. But the principal part of the population consists of independent peasants, who own their land in fee-simple. Helsingland is not cursed with the system of large landed estates which obtains farther south in Sweden, and consequently there are no *Törpare,* or cottagers, who eke out a precarious existence on small patches of land held in return for labor services rendered to the lord. The principal city is Gefle, built on a small inlet of the Gulf of Bothnia. It has a good harbor and is one of the best built towns in Sweden. Its population exceeds twenty thousand. The commerce is considerable. The exports consist of iron, timber, flax and linens. The imports are principally corn and salt. The population of Helsingland being chiefly agricultural, there are no important towns outside of Gefle. The peasants are frugal, thrifty and industrious. Their farms are small, but well kept and well cultivated, the staple produce being flax, rye and potatoes. The peasants place great pride in their neat red-painted farmhouses surrounded by patches of flowers and garden-truck. The roads are fine, and distances to market convenient.

In spite of material prosperity, however, the state of education and morals in the early part of the present century was low. Drunkenness was a common vice. Many could not read, and few indeed were those who could write. Yet in this they were no better nor no worse thån the peasantry of other European countries at the time, for the day of modern public schools had not yet arrived. But with the advent of Devotionalism and temperance reform a radical change took place. The people began to read and turned to habits of industry and sobriety.

It was the best part of the population which joined the Devotionalists, namely, the peasants and independent artisans. Some of the clergy, too, became interested and took part in the conventicles. But Jonas Olson continued to be the leader and the principal lay-member. He enjoyed the respect and the confidence of the entire community, representing it in a public capacity as juror to the district court. For seventeen years Jonas Olson and the Devotionalists of Helsingland assembled in conventicles and read their Bibles and books of devotion unmolested, enjoying their full privileges as members of the Established Church, when a new actor appeared upon the scene. This actor was Eric Janson.

II.—The Rise of Jansonism.

Eric Janson[1] was born December 19, 1808, in Biskopskulla Parish, Uppland, and was the second son in a family of four sons and one daughter. His father, Johannes Mattson, was a poor man, who by thrift and industry succeeded in laying by enough means to become the owner of a small landed estate in Österunda Parish, Westmanland, where Eric spent the formative period of his youth. Eric Janson was a born religious leader. He was not a profound speculator, but was endowed with a rare gift of eloquence and an extraordinary power to control the actions of large bodies of men. Little is known of his youth, except that his education was meagre, consisting merely of the religious instruction required in a catechumen of the Established Church. While yet a mere boy he experienced the call of religion, but soon suffered a relapse, and there was nothing in his mode of life to distinguish him from the pleasure-loving youth of the social class to which he belonged.

---

[1] This surname is a modified form of Johannes, the baptismal name of Eric's father.

At the age of twenty-six he experienced a miraculous cure from an aggravated form of rheumatism. He had for some time been suffering intense pains, but, being a man of restless, active disposition, he could not be persuaded to treat himself as an invalid. One day, as he was plowing in the fields, an unusually severe attack came upon him, in which he fainted away. On regaining consciousness, he heard a voice saying: "It is writ that whatsoever ye shall ask in prayer, believing, ye shall receive; all things are possible to him that believeth. 'If ye shall ask anything in my name, I will do it,' saith the Lord." Eric Janson recognized in the voice a message from God, and, falling upon his knees, prayed long and fervently that his lack of faith might be forgiven him and that his health might be restored. On arising, his pains had disappeared, never to return.

From this time on his whole being was turned into religious channels. He was seized with an insatiable thirst after spiritual knowledge. He read all the books of a devotional character that were to be had, but, not finding in them the peace that he longed for, turned himself towards the Bible as the sole source of spiritual comfort. His own personal experience had taught him the efficacy of faith in prayer. To want of faith, then, he ascribed all the misery and suffering which he saw about him on every hand. This want of faith he attributed to the Established Church, which was concerned more with outward churchly ceremonies than with vital piety. From the subject of faith the transition of thought to the subject of sanctification was easy and natural. After prolonged study he came to the conclusion that the Lutheran doctrine of sanctification was wrong, holding that the faithful have no sin. He seems not, however, to have advocated these views in public before 1840, for, although acting as a lay-preacher among the Devotionalists of Österunda Parish, no suspicion attached to his orthodoxy previous to that year. But in 1840 he began to preach earnestly against the assumed abuse of the devotional literature, insisting that it distracted attention from the Bible, which was the only true source of spiritual knowledge. It was not until several years later that he began to oppose in public the Lutheran doctrine of sanctification.

Up to the age of twenty-seven he remained with his parents, when, contrary to their will, he married a girl below his station. As a consequence he was thrown almost penniless upon his own resources. He rented a farm and undertook several small business ventures, in all of which he was successful, so that he was ultimately enabled to purchase the estate of Lötorp for 1000 rix-dollars, cash.

In 1842, having heard of the Devotionalists in Helsingland, he visited that province as a dealer in flour, in which capacity he traveled extensively in his own and neighboring parishes. In 1843, at the age of thirty-four, he made his second visit to Helsingland. In January of this year, while passing through Söderala Parish, he formed an acquaintance which proved to be of inestimable importance in the shaping of future events. Discovering by mere chance that Jonas Olson was a Devotionalist, he applied to him for lodging over night, and his request was hospitably granted. It was a Saturday night. The stranger appeared reserved, and had nothing to say on religious subjects. The following morning Olson's married sister came over to buy some flour. But the stranger answered, "Do you not know that to-day is the Sabbath? We will postpone business till to-morrow." The stranger accompanied the family to church. On the way home, contrary to the custom, he said not a word about the sermon. In the afternoon his host took him to a conventicle of the Devotionalists, where he was invited to speak. But he remained silent. On taking leave the following morning he said to his host, "I have had a restless night. The Lord hath imposed a duty upon me. I have struggled in prayer to avoid it, but cannot. Be a priest in your own house. I have been here a Saturday night and a Sunday night, and you have not assembled your household in prayer."

If Jonas Olson had been previously impressed by his guest's conduct, he was not any the less so now. The rebuke was accepted in humility, and from that time on Jonas Olson recognized in the stranger a man of God. He accompanied him to Hudiksval and Gefle, and everywhere introduced him to the conventicles of the Devotionalists. On account of the personal standing of his introducer, Eric Janson everywhere met with a favorable reception. Everywhere he was invited to speak, and he now no longer refused. The appreciativeness of his audiences spurred him on to his most eloquent efforts, and the evident results of his preaching convinced him that his mission as a revivalist lay in Helsingland.

In June of the same year he made his third visit to Helsingland. He was now in such demand that, like his great Master, he was obliged to travel by night and preach by day. His sermons frequently lasted from five to six hours. Many of the clergy visited his meetings, but as yet no objections were raised to his preaching. His fourth journey to Helsingland was made in the following autumn. He now decided to sell his estate in Westmanland and move to Helsingland. In the meantime, however, his father died, and he moved instead into the home thus left vacant. Here he remained till April, 1844, when he accomplished his original purpose and removed to Forsa in the north of Helsingland.

With the advent of Eric Janson to Helsingland in 1842 we may, roughly speaking, say that Jansonism begins. Eric Janson never had any large following in his own province of Westmanland, nor even in his own parish. Although, indeed, he made numerous converts outside of Helsingland, this province nevertheless remained the Jansonist stronghold. The reason is to be sought in the fact that the conditions in Helsingland were particularly favorable for the reception of his doctrine. To the Devotionalists of Helsingland there was nothing positively new in his teaching. The two points in which he disagreed with the Established Church were, firstly, with regard to the doctrine of sanctification; secondly, with regard to the devotional literature. In the doctrine of sanctification he agreed with the Methodists, holding that the faithful have no sin. But, as we have seen, Jonas Olson had accepted this doctrine from George Scott, the English Methodist clergyman stationed in Stockholm. It is impossible to ascertain whether or not Eric Janson himself ever came under the personal influence of George Scott. Some of his followers assert that he did; others assert with equal positiveness that he did not. But be that as it may, in matters of faith he had much in common with John Wesley, and his style of preaching and method of delivery is said to have resembled very much that of the early Methodists. Nor was his rejection of the devotional literature new in Helsingland. In 1805, Eric Stålberg, of the parish of Piteå, had founded a sect of Separatists, which spread rapidly over the greater part of Norrland, including the province of Helsingland. One characteristic of this sect was that, with the exception of Luther's writings, it discouraged the use of devotional literature, saying that, at the best, human writings are full of error and only tend to distract the attention from the Word of God. Although Jonas Olson and the majority of the orthodox Devotionalists in Helsingland cannot be said to have shared this view previous to the advent of Eric Janson, they were nevertheless familiar with it.

Jansonism did not spring ready-made from the brain of its author. It was a gradual development, and the form which it ultimately assumed was largely determined by the attitude of the Established Church. Eric Janson did not at first display any separatistic tendencies. He merely preached against the rationalism and dead orthodoxy which were prevalent in the Swedish Church. He advocated a return to the simplicity and earnestness of primitive Christianity. He warned his followers to read the Word of God, and did not hesitate to punish in public the sins of prominent individuals. His preaching was of a pre-eminently nomistic character, and many even of those who thought they had found peace in God saw the vanity of their lives. He traveled from parish to parish conducting revival meetings. The number of his adherents was soon estimated at from 1500 to 4000. The clergy became alarmed at the rapid growth of a strong religious sentiment over which they had no control and the import of which they did not understand. They regarded the Jansonists as a new sect holding doctrines that were subversive of the existing church organization. In order to regain their lost hold upon their congregations they denounced Janson from the pulpit, and appeared in the conventicles to warn their parishioners against the impostor and false prophet. They attempted to refute his heresies with regard to the devotional literature and the doctrine of sanctification. But Janson was gifted with a matchless power of debate, besides being well versed in the Scriptures, and whenever it came to a battle of words was almost certain to come off victorious. The Jansonists were refused admittance to the Lord's Supper. Eric Janson retaliated by saying that there could be no faith without persecution; that there was no saving power in the sermon of an unconverted minister; and forbade his followers to worship in the Established Church, holding his conventicles at the time of the regular church service. This was the beginning of his estrangement from the Established Church.

As the influence of Janson increased, so also the number and hostility of his enemies. His followers were subjected to the abuse and insult of the rabble. Their meetings were disturbed, their houses pelted with stones, and their persons assaulted. But they praised the Lord who tried their faith by allowing them to be persecuted. They marched along the public highways at night and sang spiritual hymns, or gathered in front of the parsonages to pray for the conversion of their unregenerate pastors. When their conventicles were prohibited they assembled in the woods and in out of the way places to partake of the Holy Communion. Faint rumors of these midnight gatherings came to the church authorities, and the spectre of a new peasant insurrection stalked abroad. Eric Janson was regarded as a second Thomas Münzer. He was charged with all sorts of atrocious crimes. A large number of his followers were women. Women frequently accompanied him on his missionary journeys. With one of these, by the name of Sophia Schön, he was particularly accused of sustaining improper relations. One night she was surprised in her home by the pastor of Österunda Parish, who had come with a number of his henchmen to find Eric Janson. Eric Janson was, of course, not to be found; but Sophia Schön was dragged from her bed and brought, dressed only in her linen, to the sheriff's bailiff.

In June, 1844, an event took place which gave the opponents of the new heresy an opportunity of adopting severe legal measures. Already since 1840 Eric Janson had witnessed against the assumed abuse of the devotional literature. The human writings of Luther, Arndt, Scriver, Nohrborg had usurped the place of the Bible. These new idols had stolen away the hearts of the people. They must be destroyed.

The burning of the books took place June 11. A great concourse of people from the country around assembled on a farm near the town of Tranberg. An immense bonfire was made of books, pamphlets, tracts—everything except the Bible, the hymn-book and catechism. Amidst the singing of hymns and great spiritual exaltation the assemblage watched the destruction of the "Harlot of Babylon."

The embers of the fire had hardly died out before the news was spread in every quarter of Sweden. People were horrified. Two days later, Janson was arrested by the Crown officials and brought before the sheriff's court in Gefle. After a preliminary trial he was transferred to the sheriff's court in Westerås, under whose jurisdiction he properly belonged. Here his mental condition was examined into by a medical expert, while a court chaplain examined into his spiritual. He was finally released to await a new trial, but was not allowed to return to Helsingland.

In the meantime, delegations of his adherents had visited the king, and had been promised a hearing of their grievances before the proper authorities. Upon his release Janson himself sought admission to the king, and was so graciously received that he wrote back to his friends, "I have triumphed at court." In September, 1844, he was summoned to appear before court in Westerås. In his defense he stated that the Church had abused its trust; that it had fallen from the true faith; that its servants were mere worldlings; that he was sent by God to restore the faith and show sinners the way of salvation. He was released and allowed a pass to his home in Forsa, in Helsingland.

In the meantime, the ardor of his adherents in Helsingland had not abated. Jansonism was being preached in every quarter. The reappearance of the leader gave a new impetus to the movement. His enemies had not been able to do him any injury. The king and the highest secular authorities in the realm were his sympathizers. It was only the hierarchy of the Established Church that sought his destruction. But full amnesty might soon be expected, the abominable machinations of the Church would be thwarted, the dawn of religious freedom was not far distant. So thought his simple-minded followers. His journey through Helsingland was one continued ovation. Everywhere the people flocked to the conventicles. Those who were left in doubt by his preaching were converted by the magnetic touch of his hand. In some parishes the churches remained almost empty.

October 28, 1844, the second crusade against religious books took place—this time is Söderala Parish—and now not even the hymn-book and the catechism were spared. Janson was immediately arrested. But there was reason to be cautious. He was again released to await a new trial. Hardly had he been released before he was rearrested and condemned to a short imprisonment for holding revival meetings. December 18 he was summoned before the House of Bishops in Upsala. His case was not decided.

It would be neither profitable nor interesting to rehearse the legal chicanery and petty persecution with which his life was embittered, and by which he was egged on, as it were, to abandon all Lutheran traditions and assume a position of open hostility to the Established Church. Through the zeal of the inferior clergy he was arrested six times, being three times released by royal orders; twice he was admitted to the king; he was transferred from one court to another; but, it is claimed, never received a thorough and impartial investigation.

His followers were subjected to the same sort of treatment. The ancient and obsolete law against conventicles, adopted in 1726 against Hallean pietists and other heretics, was revived in all its severity. Jonas Olson and his younger brother, Olof Olson, were made to pay heavy fines for participating in the destruction of the religious books and for holding conventicles. They also were summoned before the House of Bishops in Upsala to answer for their religious opinions.

Finally, a price was put upon Eric Janson's head. He was hunted from place to place, leading a life as adventurous as even that of the sweet singer of Brandenburg in the seventeenth century. On being captured, his friends feared that he would never be released, and conspired to effect his escape. Some of them, under color of violence, took him away from the Crown official, as he was being conveyed from Gefle to Westerås, and brought him over the mountains into Norway. From there he went to Copenhagen, where, in the company of a few friends, he embarked for New York. In July, 1846, he arrived in Victoria, Knox County, Illinois, whither he had been preceded by Olof Olson.

III.—Emigration of the Jansonists and the Founding of the Bishop Hill Colony.

While hiding in the mountain fastnesses of Söderala and Alfta, Eric Janson had planned the emigration of his followers from Sweden, and the founding in America of a socialistic theocratic community, for he had by this time abandoned all hopes of obtaining in Sweden religious liberty, either for himself or for his followers. Impelled from one point to another by the spirit of opposition, he had now developed an independent system of theology, directly antagonistic to the authority of the Established Church. Without incurring the displeasure of the Church, he had begun his reformatory activity by opposing the use of the devotional literature. Then he had opposed the Lutheran doctrine of sanctification. For this, himself and his adherents had been excluded from participation in the Lord's Supper, whereupon he had dealt out the Lord's Supper with his own hands. Meeting with legal prosecution at the hands of the inferior clergy, he had rejected the authority of the Established Church altogether, and proclaimed himself as the representative of Christ, sent to restore the true Christian Church, which had disappeared from the face of the earth with the introduction of established state churches.

The central idea of Jansonism in this final stage of its development may be summed up as follows: When persecution ceased under Constantine the Great and Christianity became the state religion, Christianity became extinct. Eric Janson was sent to restore Christianity. He represented the second coming of Christ. Christ revealed himself through him, and should continue to do the same through the seed of his body. The second advent of Christ was to be more glorious than the first. "As the splendor of the second temple at Jerusalem far exceeded that of the first, erected by the son of David, so also the glory of the work which is to be accomplished by Eric Janson, standing in Christ's stead, shall far exceed that of the work accomplished by Jesus and his Apostles."[1] Eric Janson was to separate the children of God from the world and gather them into a theocratic community. In America he was to build up the New Jerusalem,

[1] Catechés. Af Eric Janson. Söderhamn, 1846, p. 80.

from whence the Gospel should go forth to all the world. The New Jerusalem should quickly extend its boundaries until it embraced all the nations of the earth. Then should the millennium be ushered in, in which Eric Janson, or the heirs of his body, should, as the representatives of Christ, reign to the end of all time.

In 1845 he had sent Olof Olson to America to examine the country and fix upon a suitable location for the community. This was before the modern Swedish emigration to the New World. America was a name almost unknown to the peasants of Helsingland. But in 1843 an adventurous Swede from the parish of Alfta had wandered as far west as Chicago. He had written home glowing accounts of the country. His letters had been circulated among friends and acquaintances, and their contents had inspired the persecuted Jansonists with a new hope. In America there was no established church; there were no inquisitorial and tyrannous priests, no supercilious aristocracy; there was a home for every one, and, above all, religious and political liberty. The Jansonists possessed a strong love of home and country, but the exile which they had formerly feared under the conventicle laws no longer appeared so terrible.

In New York, Olof Olson made the acquaintance of the Rev. Mr. Hedström, who is known as the founder of the Swedish Methodist Church in America. Hedström was stationed as a missionary among the Scandinavian seamen in New York. He held his services in a dismantled vessel, a part of which was fitted up for the reception of Olof Olson's family, consisting of his wife and two children, who remained there during the winter of 1845–6. Under the influence of Hedström, Olof Olson joined the Methodist communion, and presently proceeded on his way to Victoria, Knox County, Illinois, where he was hospitably received by Hedström's brother. After a prospecting tour of Illinois, Wisconsin and Minnesota, Olof Olson wrote back to Sweden confirming previous favorable reports of the country, and recommending Illinois as the future place of settlement. In July of 1846 he was joined by Eric Janson, and together they fixed upon a point in Henry County as the location of the settlement. Olof Olson, however, never joined the community, but purchased a farm near Victoria, where he died shortly after the arrival of the main body of the Jansonists.

Before leaving Sweden, Eric Janson had appointed certain trustworthy men to conduct the emigration. Chief among these were Jonas Olson, Olof Johnson, Andreas Berglund, and Olof Stenberg, all of whom were to play an important part in the later history of the Jansonists.

While the orthodox Devotionalists in Helsingland consisted chiefly of independent farmers and artisans, the Jansonists included in their number a large proportion of miners and factory hands, and poor people of every description, for Jansonism was, in the true sense of the word, a popular religious movement. Many of the Jansonists were therefore persons who were unable to defray the expenses of a long journey. It was this fact which prompted Eric Janson to make community of goods a part of the social economy of the New Jerusalem. He based his reasons for the adoption of communism entirely on scriptural grounds. Neither he nor his followers knew any other form of communism than that based on religion. The Jansonists were unacquainted with the philosophical systems of the great social reformers of France. The politico-economic questions that were agitating the proletariat in the great world without had left them undisturbed. They were illiterate people. Their reading was limited to one book, but in that book they found that the first Christian church had taken care of its poor and that material goods had been held in common. So the wealthy sold their property, real as well as personal, and the proceeds went to the common coffers to be added to the widow's mite. The sums which were thus contributed ranged from 24,000 crowns downward, and were paid over to the men in charge of the emigration.

When the time for the emigration arrived it was found that 1100 Jansonists were willing to abandon their homes for the sake of religion. It was impossible to secure passage at one and the same time for so many people, for the Swedish vessels which touched at American ports were limited in number and were merely freight vessels without accommodations for passengers. So the emigrants were dispatched in parties as opportunity offered. The vessels were small, rooming only from fifty to one hundred and fifty passengers apiece. Many of them were unseaworthy, and not unfrequently they were overloaded. One was lost at sea, another was shipwrecked off the coast of Newfoundland, and still another occupied five months in the voyage.

The emigrants gathered in Göteborg, Söderhamn and Stockholm, but by far the greatest number sailed from Gefle. The first vessel to set sail from Gefle left in the summer of 1846. For weeks previous to the departure of the vessel vehicles of every description came trundling into the seaboard town of Gefle. From a distance of over a hundred miles pedestrians came in travel-stained and foot-sore. A feverish excitement reigned. No one wanted to be left behind, for the Jansonists believed that when they should stand out to sea Sweden would be destroyed for the iniquity of the Established Church. It was a sad parting. Families were torn asunder, children left their parents, husbands left their wives, the mother left her infant in the cradle. It was the flower of the youth that went, principally young men and women between the ages of twenty-five and thirty-five. Their friends never expected to hear of them again. It was feared that they would be taken by pirates, or that the captains of their vessels would sell them into slavery, or bring them to the terrible "island" of Siberia where the Czar of Russia sends all his desperate criminals. In American waters, too, there were frightful sea-monsters, more ferocious and destructive than even the Midgard serpent. And if America was the home of freedom and a country of fabulous wealth, it was also the resort of cut-throats and assassins and full of tropical abnormities.

Everything was ready for the departure when, at the very last moment, the passports were withheld by the authorities. However, a delegation of the Jansonists, headed by Jonas Olson, waited upon King Oscar I., who gave them an order for the necessary papers.

The first shipload of passengers was met in New York by Eric Janson, who had proceeded from Victoria to meet them. From Troy the emigrants went by canal to Buffalo, thence by way of the Great Lakes to Chicago. In Chicago they purchased horses and wagons for the conveyance of the invalids and the baggage. The able-bodied walked on foot one hundred miles across the unbroken prairie to Victoria, where the party arrived in July, 1846. A few days later the Jansonists removed to Red Oak Grove, about three miles west of the present Bishop Hill, where for two hundred and fifty dollars their leader had purchased an improved eighty-acre farm in section nine of Weller Township. August 2 one hundred and sixty acres of land in section eight of the same township were purchased for $1100. This was a very desirable piece of property, containing not only cultivated fields, but also a log-cabin and outhouses.

It now remained to choose a suitable town-site. The southeast quarter of section fourteen, township fourteen, was finally decided upon, and purchased of the United States government, September 26, for $200. It was a beautiful spot, sparsely covered with a small growth of oak trees, and located on the south bank of the South Edward Creek. On the same day two additional quarters were purchased in sections twenty-three and twenty-four of the same township for $400.

Anticipating the arrival of the second party of immigrants, two log-houses and four large tents were erected, all of which were in readiness when Jonas Olson arrived with his party on the 28th of October. Simultaneously with the setting in of cold weather, when the tents had to be vacated, a new party arrived. Several log cabins were hastily put together, and a large sod house erected, which latter served as a common kitchen and dining-hall. Twelve "dug-outs," about twenty-five or thirty feet long and eighteen feet wide, were also built. In these dug-outs two tiers of beds were placed along each wall, and each bed held two or more occupants. In one dug-out there were three tiers of beds and three occupants in each bed, fifty-two unmarried women performing their toilets there morning and evening. The mud caves were damp and unwholesome, and the mortality was frightful. Nearly every morning a fresh corpse would be pulled out from the reeking death-traps. Before the snow fell a fourth party of immigrants had arrived, and four hundred persons wintered in the settlement, of whom seventy were stationed at Red Oak Grove.

One of the first concerns of the Jansonists was to provide a place of worship. Already before the arrival of the second party a large tabernacle had been erected. It was built in the form of a cross and was able to room about a thousand persons. The material consisted of logs and canvas, and the whole structure was intended merely as a temporary makeshift. Divine worship was held here twice a day on week days and three times on Sundays. Eric Janson himself went the rounds of the camp at five o'clock in the morning to call the people to devotion. Half an hour later the services began, and frequently lasted for two hours. The second devotional meeting was held in the evening. When spring arrived, however, and the work in the fields began, the morning and evening devotions were substituted by a short meeting during the noon recess, and in favorable weather this was frequently conducted in the open air.

The Jansonists were illiterate people, but they held progressive views with regard to elementary education. Already the first winter, at such times when the weather prevented out-door work, a school for adults was carried on in the tabernacle by Mrs. Hebbe and, later, Mr. Hellström, who both instructed in the advanced arts of writing and ciphering. A similar school for adults was established at Red Oak. As early as January, 1847, an English school was opened. A Presbyterian clergyman, the Rev. Mr. Talbot, taught some thirty-five children in a mud-cave from January to July. At times he was assisted by his two daughters and by Mrs. Pollock, who was a member of the community. Mr. Talbot was succeeded by Nelson Simons, M. D.

Measures were also taken for the propaganda of faith. Eric Janson appointed twelve young men to be the apostles of Jansonism in the New World. Great expectations were centered in these twelve young men. After a few months' instruction in the English language, they were sent out upon their mission to convert the United States and the world. They met with but moderate success, however, for the Yankee was too busy inventing bad clocks and peddling cheap tinware to listen to what the missionaries had to say.

The community experienced great difficulty in securing sufficient food. After the expenses of the journey and the purchase of so much land, the funds of the society were well nigh exhausted, and credit they had none. The grain had to be hauled twenty-eight miles to the nearest mill to be ground. But the mill was constantly under repairs and could not be relied upon. After attempting to supply their wants by means of hand-mills, the society erected a small grist-mill on the Edwards Creek, which, when the water failed, was run by horse-power.

In the spring of 1847 the community began to manufacture adobe. Several houses were built of this material, some of which remained standing until 1862. The ravine which intersected the town-site contained chalkstone in abundance, and the preparation of it into cement was taught the Jansonists by Philip Mauk. The first frame building was also erected in 1847, the lumber being hauled from Red Oak

Grove, where a sawmill, run by horse-power, had been put up by the society. As the needs of the society increased, this mill was later on bartered away for a larger one run by water-power. May 4, 1848, the society purchased of Cramer and Wilsie forty acres of land for $1500. This land was excellent timber land, and contained a sawmill more than large enough to supply all the wants of the society.

While the Jansonists had been employed in these building operations they had not neglected agriculture. The land at Red Oak Grove had been put under cultivation, and pieces of land had been rented here and there, for which they were obliged to pay one-third of the gross produce. During the first year the Jansonists broke three hundred and fifty acres of land and laid three and a half miles of sod fence. In the autumn of the year their threshing was done by Mr. Broderick, whose machine they purchased, only to make it serve as a model for a larger and more improved machine of their own make.

November 18, one hundred acres of land in section seventeen, Weller Township, were purchased of W. H. Griffins for three hundred and eighty dollars.

June 4, 1847, the fifth party of Jansonists arrived. The party contained, besides children, four hundred adults. This accretion to the community required the purchase of more land. Before the close of the year the following purchases had been made: eighty acres in section seventeen, two hundred and forty acres in section sixteen, thirty-nine acres belonging to Mr. Broderick, besides other property.

In January of the following year an old-fashioned wind grist-mill was erected, the mill on the Edwards Creek proving inadequate to meet the increasing demands made upon it.

With the arrival of the new party a great scarcity of dwelling room arose. Five new mud-caves were excavated for the people, while similar provisions were made for the horses and cattle. Nevertheless the Jansonists suffered intensely. The winter was a severe one. The dug-outs were damp and unwholesome and fearfully crowded. The ravine into which they faced was alternately swept by fierce wind storms or choked up with snow. There was lack of provisions, and the Jansonists suffered from hunger as well as from cold. The change of climate also produced suffering. Fevers, chills and diarrhœa were common, and many succumbed. The hardships were more than many members of the community had the resolution to bear, and they left singly and in squads as their lack of faith and pressing wants seemed to require. The seeds of internal discord, too, were sown, for religious differences arose which resulted in the withdrawal of about two hundred members in the autumn of 1848. The majority, however, remained steadfast. Their courage was cheered by the matchless eloquence of their leader, and their unshakable faith in him helped them to surmount all difficulties.

In the summer of 1848 the Jansonists began to manufacture kiln-dried brick, the kilns being located about one mile west of the settlement. A four-story brick house one hundred by forty-five feet was erected, which, in 1851, was extended one hundred feet. The basement was arranged into a common dining-hall and kitchen, whereas the upper stories were divided into dwelling apartments. At the same time, several frame tenement houses and some additional houses of adobe were erected. In this year also the Old Colony Church, a large frame edifice, the upper part of which was designed to serve as a church, while the basement was arranged into tenements, was begun and completed in the following year, the tabernacle having been previously destroyed by fire.

With improved dwellings came improved health. Even those who had to remain in the mud-caves were better off, because they were no longer so crowded, and they found, in the summer-time at least, plenty of exercise in the open air. For there were no drones in this hive. The incentive to work, which one should suppose had been removed with the removal of individual property, was supplied by religion. They were no longer working for their own advancement, but for the glory of God. Had He not led them, as He had led the people of Israel, to a new Canaan? They were His chosen people. In them His wonderful designs for the regeneration of the world were to be fulfilled. Their city was the refuge of the faithful; it was the New Jerusalem. So they reclaimed the prairie and subdued the forest to further the kingdom of God. Their labor was not in vain. The earth gave forth bountifully of its harvests and prosperity attended upon them.

Their methods of agriculture were laborious, but as their means improved, and as they learned the ways of the country of their adoption, they became as expert as any in the use of improved machinery. In the autumn of 1847 they harvested their grain in the Swedish fashion with the scythe. In 1848 they introduced cradles, and, in 1849, reapers. In order to secure the harvest of 1848 thirty cradle-scythes were kept going day and night, until it was discovered that the night work endangered the health, when eighteen hours were made to constitute a day's work. The young men wielded the cradles—and wonderful feats were performed with the cradle in those days—while the middle-aged men and the women bound the sheaves; boys and girls gathered the sheaves together, while the old men placed them in shocks. In the evening, when the day's work was done and the harvesters were retiring from the field, an interesting spectacle presented itself to the observer. Two by two, in a long procession a couple of hundred strong, the harvesters wended their homeward way, first the men carrying their cradle-scythes over their shoulders, then the women with their hand-rakes, and, finally, the children, all singing some merry harvest-song of their native country, while keeping step to the music. On arriving at the village they repaired to the common dining hall, where a bounteous repast awaited them on long wooden tables, some of which were set aside for the men, others for the women, and still others for the children.

Another important industry of the community was the cultivation of flax. This was the staple industry in the province of Helsingland, and the Jansonists were thoroughly familiar with every branch of it. Already the first year they put part of their fields under cultivation for flax. They also helped the neighboring farmers, who cultivated the plant merely for the sake of the seed, to harvest their crops, and received the straw in payment for their work. From the crop of 1847 they manufactured 12,473 yards of linen and carpet matting, for all of which they found a ready sale. The volume of manufacture continued to increase till 1851, when it reached 30,579 yards of linen and carpeting. After this it decreased till 1857, when it ceased altogether, except for home consumption, the new railroad enabling the eastern manufacturers to flood the market with their wares and drive out competition. The aggregate amount of linen sold to 1857 was 130,309 yards and of carpeting 22,569 yards. To this must be added the no inconsiderable quantities consumed at home in order to arrive at the total amount of manufacture. The spinning and weaving were done exclusively by women, children of both sexes assisting at spooling and other light work. In the early years when looms were scarce the weavers were divided into squads and the looms kept running night and day.

The sixth party of immigrants arrived in 1849, and consisted of Swedish and Norwegian converts under the leadership of the Jansonist missionary Nylund. Between La Salle and Chicago the party was attacked by the Asiatic cholera. Arrived in Chicago in a pitiable condition, the party was met by a member of the community, who conducted it to Bishop Hill. Thus the dread disease was transplanted to the society, and, breaking out on the 22d day of July, raged without intermission till the middle of September. It carried away one hundred and forty-three persons in the prime of life. The excessive mortality was due partly to improper treatment, the fever-parched patients being, according to the old medical superstition, not allowed to touch water. Some of the Jansonists removed to the neighborhood of La Grange, where the community possessed some real property, but, finding themselves still pursued by the fell destroyer, fled in vain to an island in the Mississippi, where Eric Janson's wife and one child were among the victims.

In 1850 another party arrived under the leadership of Olof Stenberg, who was returning from a business visit to Sweden. Stenberg's party was attacked by the Asiatic cholera between Buffalo and Milwaukee. The party consisted of one hundred and sixty persons. On account of stress of weather and a breakage in the machinery, the voyage by steamer occupied no less than two weeks. The provisions gave out and the passengers suffered famine as well as disease. Many were buried in the waters of Lake Michigan, and many died in the lazaretto at Milwaukee. The leader has been accused of criminal negligence with regard to the performance of certain duties, but on the evidence of surviving members of his party the charge is without foundation.

Later in the same year still another party arrived; it consisted of eighty persons. The tenth party consisted of seventy persons and arrived in 1854. Besides these larger accretions, converts joined the society singly and in groups, and continued to do so up to a late date.

It was now a little over three years since the village of Bishop Hill had sprung into existence. It took its being eleven years after the first white man's habitation had been erected in the country which came to be organized as Henry County, and nine years after that organization had taken place. Previous to it there existed, besides some others, the infant settlements of Andover, Genesceo, Wethersfield, and La Grange, the products of a strange mixture of New England philanthropy and speculation. But from the very day of its foundation, Bishop Hill assumed the chief place among the settlements in Henry County. From 1846 to 1850, in the purchase of land and the necessaries of life, it put between

$10,000 and $15,000 in gold into circulation, which was a matter of extreme importance at a time when business was principally conducted by barter, and when the only money in use was paper money valued at a few cents on the dollar. In 1850 its population had swelled to over one thousand, while the entire population of the county, an area of eight hundred and thirty square miles, was only three thousand, eight hundred and seven. If the labor value of an immigrant may be capitalized at ten hundred dollars, then the Jansonists had in their persons alone brought one million dollars into the country. Nearly every province in Sweden was represented in the community at Bishop Hill, and the Jansonists' letters home concerning the new country paved the way for that mighty tide of Swedish immigration which in a few years began to roll in upon Illinois and the Northwest, and which in 1882 culminated in a grand total for the year of 64,607 souls. For nine successive years, from 1878 to 1886, there arrived annually from the native land of the Jansonists more immigrants than from France or Italy or Austria or Russia, or any country save only Great Britain and Germany.

But while the Norns were weaving the fabric of history, the Jansonists were building their village and improving the resources of the wilderness. In 1850 they owned in fee simple or possessed an equitable interest in about fourteen hundred acres of land, which were partially under cultivation for wheat, flax and corn, and partly set aside for the pasturage of large herds of horses and cattle. The village of Bishop Hill, named after *Biskopskulla*, the birthplace of Eric Janson, consisted of several large brick houses, all of which, with the exception of one, were of adobe, a number of log and frame buildings, and seventeen dug-outs, together with storehouses, barns and outhouses of every description. It contained at least the nuclei of a store, a blacksmith shop, and all the other appurtenances of a modern Western city. At the head of the community—at the head of the industrial army of one thousand busy workmen—was one supreme director. Eric Janson was the temporal as well as spiritual ruler. He appointed the superintendents of departments and the foremen of gangs. Nothing was undertaken without his sanction. He represented the community in business on the markets in Chicago and St. Louis. Property was bought and sold in his name or in the name of agents appointed by him. The society was, indeed, still struggling with poverty and debt, but the primary conditions of prosperity were nevertheless manifestly present.

IV.—The Adventurer John Root and the Murder of Eric Janson.

In the autumn of 1848 there arrived in Bishop Hill an adventurer by the name of John Root. He was the son of well-to-do parents in Stockholm, and a man of education, refinement of manners and pleasing address. For some unknown reason he had emigrated from Sweden. As a soldier in the United States army he had taken part in the Mexican campaign. After receiving his discharge at the close of the war he found his way to Bishop Hill. He was received with open arms by Eric Janson and the society, and was presently admitted as a member. He soon fell in love with a cousin of Eric Janson and applied to him for her hand in marriage. The request was granted, it being stipulated, however, that if Root should ever wish to leave the society, it was to be optional with his wife whether to accompany him or not. A written document to this effect was drawn up and duly signed by the contracting parties. It soon became apparent that the new member was not fitted for a religious communistic society. He was opposed to serious labor, and spent his time in the chase, with his gun on his shoulder and his bowie-knife in his belt. But tiring even of this employment, he sought new adventures as interpreter and guide to a Hebrew peddler. The Jew was never heard of again; but a few years after the decomposed body of a murdered man was discovered under the floor of a deserted cabin some miles from Bishop Hill. After an absence of several months, during which time his wife gave birth to a child, John Root returned. Very soon he proposed to his wife that they leave the society, to which she strenuously objected. Eric Janson supported Mrs. Root in her determination to remain, which exasperated Root to such an extent that he threatened the lives of both Mrs. Root and Eric Janson. Perceiving that he could neither persuade nor frighten his wife into submission, he determined to carry her away by force. Obtaining the aid of a young man by the name of Stanley, he drove into Bishop Hill one day while the members of the community were at dinner, and, rushing into his wife's apartment, caught her up in his arms and carried her to the vehicle in waiting. The alarm was given, however, and the fugitives were hotly pursued. Two miles from the village they were overtaken by a dozen sturdy Jansonists on horseback and compelled to halt. The rescuers explained that if Mrs. Root wished to leave the community she was at liberty to do so; but if she desired to remain they proposed to take her back, by force, if need be. Meanwhile Root and Stanley, being both armed, kept the rescuing party at bay. But at this juncture Mrs. Root, who, together with her child, had been placed in the bottom of the wagon, made a desperate effort to release herself. In the struggle to prevent her from so doing, Root laid his revolver on the seat behind him, where it was immediately snatched by one of the rescuing party. Stanley promptly surrendered, and Mrs. Root was brought back to the village in triumph. Thwarted in his purpose of forcible abduction, Root had recourse to the law, and swore out a warrant for the arrest of Eric Janson and others, on the charge of restraining the liberty of his wife. Mrs. Root was subpœnaed as a witness. The officer who was charged with the execution of the summons insisted upon her accompanying him at once. He took her to Cambridge, where she was illegally confined in a room and denied communication with her friends. Here Root got possession of his wife a second time, and spirited her away to the Rock River settlement. Thence he took her to Davenport, and finally to Chicago, where he had a sister living. The sister, disapproving of Root's conduct, communicated with the Jansonists at Bishop Hill, and Eric Janson sent a delegation to Chicago to offer Mrs. Root safe-conduct to the community. A place was designated where at a given time she might meet her friends. Knowing the desperate character of Root and anticipating a hot pursuit, men had been stationed with relays of horses at intervals along the road from Chicago to Bishop Hill, and the distance of one hundred and fifty miles was accomplished without a single stop.

When Root found that his wife had escaped, his rage knew no bounds. Baffled in his attempt to overtake her, he proceeded to the Rock River settlement, whence he returned to Bishop Hill, at the head of a mob. The mob terrorized the village for a few days, but finding neither Mrs. Root nor the principal agents in her abduction, presently dispersed. This was in the latter part of March, 1850. In the following week, on the evening of April 1, Root returned at the head of a second mob, angrier and more formidable than the first. A veteran of the Mexican war had been robbed of his wife, who was held in duress by a set of communists, for what vile purpose no one knew. It was only six years since the hateful Mormons had been expelled and their city and temple well-nigh razed to the ground; what was to hinder that this new Nauvoo should likewise be wiped off from the face of the earth? The rough, but justice-loving frontiersmen poured into the encampment at Buck Grove, half a mile from Bishop Hill, until the mob grew to the proportions of an army. The village was surrounded and communication with the outside world shut off. For three days the Regulators hesitated to begin the work of destruction. Janson was hid in an artificial cave out on the prairie, Olson was absent on business in Andover—all the principal participants in the affair between Root and his wife had been spirited away. When the attempt was finally made to burn the village, the mob was met by an armed posse of the neighboring settlers, who had come to the relief of the community. The mob, seeing that it would have to encounter a desperate resistance, allowed itself to be persuaded of the innocent character of the society, and dispersed without having done any serious injury.

During these critical times the Jansonists bore themselves with fortitude, as befitted a religious people. Indeed, splendid displays of heroism were not wanting. Thus, Nils Hellbom committed an act of deliberate and premeditated bravery which might easily have cost him his life. The story of it is told as follows: "The mob had surreptitiously introduced a tall Indian into the woods. It is the Indian custom to remove the hair together with the scalp from an enemy's head, thus suffering him to die a lingering death in great pain. The Indian in question had been secretly instructed to destroy Jonas Olson in this manner, for Jonas Olson had been the chief agent in assisting Root's wife to escape. Nils Hellbom, who is a fearless boatswain, large and strong, weight two hundred and twenty-five pounds, hearing of this, dressed himself in a Swedish sheepskin greatcoat, having the woolly side out, so that only his rolling eyeballs were visible. Then going out to where the Indian was, edged up to him and said in Swedish, 'What do you want? Do you want my scalp, too?'" The Indian's ignorance of the Swedish language alone prevented the shedding of blood.

While the mob was raging at Bishop Hill, Eric Janson had succeeded in making good his escape to St. Louis, being accompanied by his wife, Mrs. John Root and others. In St. Louis he remained until all danger was past, when he returned to Bishop Hill. His trial was to come off at the May term of the Henry County Circuit Court in Cambridge. He seems to have had a presentiment that he should never return from that trial. In the last sermon that he preached in Bishop Hill he told his followers that he should die a martyr to religion. It was the most powerful sermon that he had ever preached. Strong men wept and the community was full of evil foreboding. The last public act of his life was to distribute the Lord's Supper, and in so doing he repeated these words of the Holy Writ, "I will not drink henceforth of this fruit of the vine, until that day when I drink it new in my father's kingdom." On Monday morning, Mr. Maskel, an employe of the community, called at Janson's dwelling-place with a horse and buggy to take him to Cambridge. On coming down the steps Janson said, "Well, Mr. Maskel, will you stop the bullet for me to-day?"—which the latter cheerfully agreed to do. It was the 13th day of May, 1850. The court had adjourned for the noon recess. Janson was standing by a window in the court-room, while his counsel was sitting at a table engaged in writing. Suddenly John Root appeared in the doorway, calling Eric Janson by name. As Janson turned round, his eye met the gleam of a pistol-barrel, and a bullet struck him full in the heart; as he fell, a second bullet grazed his shoulder. It is impossible now to ascertain the further particulars of the murder. Root's friends maintain that he and Janson had been conversing through the open window, and that Janson had uttered some insulting remark which exasperated Root; while Janson's friends claim that the two men had not spoken to each other that day, but that Root came directly from a target practice in which he had been engaged the greater part of the forenoon.

When Eric Janson was brought home a corpse who can describe the consternation? The representative of Christ, sent to rebuild the city of God, dead! His work was but just begun! It was beyond human comprehension. But the ways of God are wonderful. Might he not recall his servant to life? Men and women wept, and waited for the resurrection which did not come. All work, except of a merely perfunctory nature, ceased. The industrial army was demoralized, the leader was gone. Then it was that a woman stepped forward and called new life into the community.

Eric Janson's second wife was a remarkable woman. Left an orphan at an early age, she was adopted by a well-to-do family in Göteborg, who brought her with them to New York at the age of fifteen. Her first husband was a sailor, who went out to sea and never returned. Her second husband gave her an education, and she, in return, assisted him as teacher in a private school, of which he was the principal. As Mrs. Pollock, she became acquainted with Olaf Olson in 1845, through her pastor, the Rev. Mr. Hedström. When the main body of the Jansonists arrived in 1848 she met for the first time Eric Janson, who had come to receive them. She became converted, and followed the Jansonists to Bishop Hill, for Janson preached that there was no salvation outside the New Jerusalem. Her husband, who loved her as he did his life, went with her and tried to persuade her to return. But for the sake of her soul she dared not, and her husband died of a broken heart in Victoria. Mrs. Pollock lost her reason over her husband's death, but shortly recovered. Marrying again, she became Mrs. Gabrielson. Gabrielson died of the cholera, leaving one son, who grew to be a young man. During a large part of her stay in the community she had taught in the community's school, and her knowledge of English had frequently been of service to the Jansonists. She was still an exceedingly handsome woman, composed and dignified in speech and deportment. Having in the meantime become a widower, Eric Janson took her to wife. As Mrs. Janson she superintended the work of the women, and, moreover, acted as her husband's secretary. She had been married but a few months at the time of Janson's death, but nevertheless she knew more about the affairs of the community than any other person in it. So, the rightful heir to Janson's authority, namely, his son by his first wife, being but a mere boy, Mrs. Janson took the reins of government into her own hands.

But among the Jansonists women were not allowed to speak in public. Andreas Berglund was therefore appointed to be the nominal guardian of Eric Janson's son. In spiritual matters his authority was absolute, but in matters pertaining to business no important step was taken without the knowledge and consent of Mrs. Janson.

For three days Janson's body lay in state. On the day of the funeral the Old Colony Church was crowded to suffocation. Janson had gained many friends outside the community among those with whom he had had business relations. Strangers, too, there were who came to satisfy a wanton curiosity. The services were opened with song and prayer. Then Mrs. Janson stepped forward, and, in the presence of the congregation, placed her hand upon Berglund's bowed head, creating him guardian of the heir to the leadership of God's chosen people until such time when the boy should have reached the age of majority. After the funeral sermon, which was preached by Andreas Berglund, an oration in the English language, together with several other addresses, the body was escorted to the community's burying-ground. There was no muffled music, no display of shining uniforms, no pomp of funeral trappings. The body was laid to rest in a plain wooden coffin, and a plain wooden slab marked the grave of Eric Janson, the prophet, the representative of Christ.

The death of Eric Janson may be said to have occurred at an opportune moment. He was at the height of his power. In obedience to his word, eleven hundred people had abandoned their homes in a prosperous country, to found new ones in an American wilderness. They had given up their property, had braved unknown dangers and suffered untold hardships. His power over them was extraordinary. In the terrible days of the cholera, when any of their number were stricken with the dread disease, they sought his blessing, "Go, die in peace," and, contented, dragged themselves away to their fate. But his work was accomplished. It was his to call the community into existence in spite of seemingly insurmountable difficulties; but he did not possess the administrative ability to lead it along the quiet paths of industry to economic success. As it was, he died under heroic circumstances and while the memory of his achievements was still fresh in the minds of friends and foes alike.

In person Eric Janson was tall and angular, while his face was disfigured by a deep scar across the forehead and by the abnormal prominence of his upper incisor teeth. But these defects were lost sight of in the charm of his private conversation and in the eloquence of his public address. He was a man of large social affections and, where religion did not interfere with the dictates of nature, of quick and ready sympathies. He was a man of splendid parts, and had his mind been less untrained he might possibly have become the pride and admiration of his native country, instead of ending his life before an assassin's bullet as an exile in a strange land.

V.—Jonas Olson and the Incorporation of the Bishop Hill Colony.

When the murder of Eric Janson took place in the courtroom in Cambridge, Jonas Olson was on his way to California. Being an indifferent man of business, Eric Janson had, by injudicious management, involved the community in serious financial difficulties. It was at the time when the California gold discoveries were filling the world with wonder. Their fame penetrated even to the quiet little village of Bishop Hill, and Eric Janson was carried away by the prospect of wealth easily acquired. For the immediate purpose of obtaining relief from the financial pressure resting upon the community, he dispatched, March 18, 1850, Jonas Olson with a party of eight men to California in quest of gold.

Jonas Olson was then a man past the meridian of life. He possessed no faith in the mission upon which he was sent; but although he had pleaded hard with Eric Janson to be allowed to remain at home, he was, nevertheless, obliged to go, for he was considered the man best fitted for the undertaking, and, moreover, his life was threatened at home by John Root, for his connection with the affair between the latter and his wife. After passing through innumerable hardships, as a result of which one of their number died soon after reaching California, the gold-seekers arrived in Hanktown on the eleventh day of August, 1850. Here the news reached them of Eric Janson's death. Jonas Olson did not hesitate what course of action to adopt. Next to Eric Janson he had been the principal member of the community. Among the Devotionalists in Helsingland, from whose ranks the great majority of the Jansonist converts were gained, he had been the recognized leader previous to the coming of Eric Janson. During the troublous times of religious persecution his extensive knowledge of men and affairs had more than once rescued the sinking cause of Jansonism. After the flight of their leader he had been the chief agent in effecting the emigration of the Jansonists. Now his gifts and attainments, which latter were not inconsiderable in a peasant, would once more be of service. In this conviction he immediately set out upon his return to Bishop Hill, taking with him a couple of his companions, leaving the rest to follow at their leisure. He arrived in Bishop Hill on the 8th of February, 1851.

Jonas Olson found the community under the control of Mrs. Janson and Andreas Berglund, who acted as the guardians of Eric Janson's son. During Eric Janson's lifetime no one had ventured to dispute the hereditary character of his office as spiritual and temporal leader of the community. The office was so described in the accepted doctrinal books, namely, in the hymn-book and catechism, both of which were composed by Eric Janson. During the storm and stress period of the Jansonist movement, when a strong and masterful hand was needed to bring matters to a successful issue, it is altogether probable that the question of who was to succeed Eric Janson in office had not occupied the serious attention of his followers. Every one had, as a matter of fact, submitted to the absolute authority which he assumed. On the one hand, his personality was such as to admit of no mediocre opposition. On the other, his adherents' attitude of mind predisposed them to accept any claims which he might make either for himself or for his family. He was regarded as the representative of Christ. His decisions were considered infallible, for the divine will was thought to be disclosed to him by special revelation. Upon his death, however, circumstances were greatly altered. There was very little of the dignity of divinely sanctioned authority attaching to the childish prattle before the congregation of the future official mouthpiece of God. The evil results of Janson's infallible business policy were beginning fully to manifest themselves. The guardians of Janson's son could not claim infallibility of judgment, and many of the community were dissatisfied to be governed by a woman. A respectable minority of the community, while admitting Eric Janson's other claims, were not disposed to recognize those in behalf of his heir. It was this growing sentiment of dissatisfaction which Jonas Olson voiced, when, shortly after his arrival, he denounced Andreas Berglund as a usurper and demanded his abdication. He held that Eric Janson's had been a special commission, and hence the extraordinary powers and authority incident thereto could not be inheritable. The community should not, he said, recognize any formal leader whatever, but each individual member should serve the whole according to the measure of his ability and in that capacity for which he was best fitted by nature and training. Jonas Olson's standing in the community added weight to his words, and erelong the democratic element which he represented prevailed. The movement also gained strength from the operation of another circumstance. The affairs of the community were in such a condition that a strong and able man was needed to conduct it through the impending crisis. Jonas Olson was such a man, and the community instinctively looked to him for guidance. Thus it happened that, although no formal election or transfer of power took place, the leadership quickly passed from the guardians of Eric Janson's son into the hands of Jonas Olson. With his advent into power the claims of the family of Janson retreat into the background, until upon the adoption of the charter in 1853 they practically disappear.

At the time of Janson's death the debt of the community was eight thousand dollars, which had been contracted principally in the purchase of unnecessary lands. In the summer of 1850, horses, cattle, wagons, even the crops were levied upon to satisfy the demands of the creditors. In the autumn of the year, however, the society received from various sources an accession of about eight or ten thousand dollars. A part of this money was expended in completing the brick steam flour mill, which had been begun in 1849 under the direction of Eric Janson. Soon, also, the community was able to make other improvements. An addition of one hundred feet was made to the large four-story brick tenement house. A commodious brick brewery, with a capacity of ten barrels a day, was erected for the preparation of small beer, the community's favorite beverage. Orchards were planted, and an attempt was made to raise broom-corn, which attempt succeeded so well that a contract was made to furnish a Peoria dealer with a large quantity at the remunerative price of fifty dollars a ton. The manufacture of brooms was also begun, which henceforth became a staple industry.

Under Jonas Olson's skilful management the circumstances of the community underwent a rapid and permanent improvement. But as the real and other property of the society increased, the disadvantages of not having a legal organization became apparent. It was necessary to hold property in the names of individual members, but in case of bad faith on the part of the natural heirs, complications concerning the succession might, upon the death of such members, arise in the probate courts. Hence, for the better conservation of its proprietary interests, the society decided to apply to the

State Legislature for a charter. Accordingly, on January 17, 1853, by an act of Legislature, a corporation was created, to be known as the Bishop Hill Colony.

The charter provided for a board of seven trustees, who were to hold office for life or during good behavior, but who were liable to be removed for good reasons by a majority of the male members of the colony. Vacancies in the office of trustee were to be filled in such manner as should be provided for in the by-laws. The powers of the trustees were of a most comprehensive character, enabling them generally to promote and carry out the objects and interests of the corporation, and to transact any business consistent with the benefit, support and profit of the members of the same. The business of the corporation should be manufacturing, milling, all kinds of mechanical business, agriculture, and merchandising. Furthermore, the colony might pass such by-laws concerning the government and management of its property and business, the admission, withdrawal, and expulsion of members, and the regulation of its internal policy, as it might deem proper, not inconsistent with the constitution and laws of the State.

The by-laws were adopted May 6, 1854. According to these, any person sustaining a good moral character might become a member by transferring the absolute ownership of his property to the board of trustees and subscribing to the by-laws. The trustees were empowered to decide upon the moral fitness of candidates. They might, however, in their discretion, refer the question to a vote of the adult male members. On withdrawal of membership, or expulsion from the society, a person was entitled to no compensation whatever, either for the loss of property or for time spent in the service of the community. The trustees might, however, in special cases make such recompense as they should deem proper. Any person guilty of disturbing the peace and harmony of the community, or of preaching and disseminating religious doctrines contrary to those of the Bible, might be expelled. It was to be the duty of the trustees to direct the various industrial pursuits, and generally to superintend the affairs of the community, either in person or through such agents and foremen as they might see fit to appoint. Annually, on the second Monday of January, a meeting of the adult male members was to take place for the general transaction of business. At this meeting the trustees were required to make a full and complete report of the financial condition and affairs of the society for the year ending on the Saturday next previous. Special meetings might be called by the trustees whenever the interests of the society required it. Special meetings could also be called by a majority of the adult male members, provided they signified their request to the trustees in writing five days in advance. Vacancies in the board of trustees were to be filled at an election held specially for the purpose, the person receiving the highest number of votes being elected. These by-laws might be revised, altered or amended at any regular or called meeting, by a majority of the votes cast.[1]

The adoption of the charter was a complete abandonment of the principle of hereditary leadership. It took the temporal as well as the spiritual authority out of the hands of a single individual and vested it in a board of seven trustees. In so far, the democratic movement inaugurated by Jonas Olson had found a logical conclusion. However, the popularization of the form of government was more apparent than real. According to the provisions of the by-laws, the trustees were empowered not only to regulate and direct the business and various industrial pursuits of the community, but also to decide upon the fitness of applicants for membership, as well as upon the equity of compensating retiring members. The trustees were not obliged to await the instructions of the community—only one general business meeting annually was provided for—but had the right of initiative in matters of the gravest as well as of the most trivial importance. Finally, the community had practically no check upon the trustees,

---

[1] For text of charter and by-laws see Appendix.

for they held office for life or during "good behavior," and could not be ousted before, either through criminality or gross incompetence, some serious injury had already been done.

The circumstances under which the instruments of incorporation were adopted are suggestive. The demand for the charter did not spring from the people. The majority of the community did not know what the charter meant, except that in some way it would protect their interests in court. They were told that the community would continue to be governed, not by human laws, but by the Word of God. They had no voice in the election of the trustees. The board of trustees was already made up when the petition to the Legislature asking for a charter was presented to the members of the community for their signatures. Indeed, the members were originally requested to affix their signatures, not to the petition itself, but to a blank sheet of paper, and it was only when a certain wrong-headed individual demanded to see the petition that it was given to the people for inspection at all.

On the other hand, there is no reason to suppose that the self-appointed trustees were conscious of arrogating to themselves undue powers. The Jansonists were unaccustomed to self-government. Their leaders hardly looked upon themselves as servants of the people, but rather as authoritative interpreters of the will of God. The seven trustees in question were all persons who had been appointed to positions of trust under Eric Janson, and who therefore considered that they had a perfect right to any formal recognition of the powers which they already virtually enjoyed. In reality the distribution of authority remained very much the same as it had been before. Jonas Olson continued to be the leading spirit also in the board of trustees, and his influence was sufficient to make or mar the success of any project.

VI.—Social, Economic, and Religious Life under the Charter.

Under the improved business methods made possible by the charter, the material progress of the community was rapid and permanent. The indications of prosperity became visible on all sides, especially in the improved condition of the village, which had hitherto been built without regard to any definite plan either of convenience or of beauty. The site of the village was an elevation overlooking the surrounding country, but the beauty of the spot was marred by an unsightly ravine which intersected it from north to south. During a whole summer the trustees kept men and teams at work to remove this objectionable feature, and a park was planted where the ravine had been. The new brick houses, nearly all of which were several stories in height, were erected around this park and made looking into it. When the village was completed it contained twelve brick houses, the largest of which was two hundred by four hundred and forty-five feet, and four stories in height, besides six substantial frame buildings.

The buildings were almost entirely the product of home industry. When a new building was contemplated, invitations were extended by the trustees to the members of the community to hand in plans and specifications. The bricks were burned in the society's own kilns. The lumber, a great deal of which was oak and black walnut, was sawed in the society's saw-mill, most of the iron work was forged in the society's smithy. The masonry was executed under the supervision of August Bandholtz, a German mason, who fell in love with a blue-eyed Jansonist and married into the community.

There were no fences or outhouses to break up the symmetry of the village. The streets were lined with shade trees and were kept scrupulously clean. The stables and enormous cattle-sheds were in an enclosure by themselves at some distance from the village. The village contained a general store and post-office, a smithy, a brewery, a bakery, a weaving establishment, a dye-house, and a hotel, together with wagon, furniture, harness, tailor and shoemaker shops. Besides, there were a hospital, a laundry, bath-houses, mills and manufactories. The store and post-office employed two clerks. The tailor shop employed six men and three women; the shoemaker shop, six men; the smithy, ten men; the wagon shop, six men. The smithy boasted seven forges, while the wagon shop was extensively known throughout the country for the excellent character of its work. The weaving establishment contained twelve reels and twelve hand-looms, besides which one hundred and forty spinning-wheels were distributed privately among the women of the community. The broom shop employed three men and nine women and turned out thirty dozen of brooms a day.

But, nevertheless, agriculture was the principal pursuit of the community—so much so that, in the busy seasons, work in the shop and in the manufactory was allowed to come almost to a standstill. Men, women, and children over fourteen years of age, worked side by side in the fields. Nobody who was able to work remained unemployed. The main farm was at Bishop Hill, but besides there were eight sub-farms, where gangs of workmen relieved each other at fixed intervals. A great deal of the unskilled labor was performed by women, for they constituted about two-thirds of the community, and the men were greatly needed in the trades. Unmarried women worked in the brick-kilns and assisted in the building operations, pitching the bricks, two at a time, from one story to another, instead of carrying them in hods. The milking was done wholly by women. Four women cared for the calves, four had charge of the hogs, and two worked in the dairy, where butter was made in an immense churn run by horse-power. Cheese was manufactured on a similarly extensive scale. There were eight laundresses, two dyers, four bakers and two brewers.

A visitor to the community in 1853 writes as follows:

"We had occasion this year to visit the colony and were received with great kindness and hospitality. Everything, seemingly, was on the top of prosperity. The people lived in large, substantial brick houses. We had never before seen so large a farm, nor one so well cultivated. One of the trustees took us to an adjacent hill, from which we had a view of the Colony's cultivated fields, stretching away for miles. In one place we noticed fifty young men, with the same number of horses and plows, cultivating a cornfield where every furrow was two miles in length. . . . In another place was a field of a thousand acres in broom-corn, the product of which, when baled, was to be delivered at Peoria for shipment to consignees in Boston, and was expected to yield an income of fifty thousand dollars. All the live stock was exceptionally fine and apparently given the best of care. There was a stable of more than one hundred horses, the equals to which it would be hard to find. One morning I was brought to an enclosure on the prairie where the cows were being milked. There must have been at least two hundred of them, and the milkmaids numbered forty or fifty. There was a large wagon, in which an immense tub was suspended, and in this tub each girl, ascending by means of a step-ladder, emptied her pail. The whole process was over in half an hour. On Sunday I attended service. There was singing and praying, and the sermon, by one of the leaders, contained nothing that a member of any Christian denomination might not hear in his own church. Altogether I retain the most agreeable remembrance of this visit."[1]

The common dining-halls and kitchen were located in a large brick building at the northwest corner of the public square. The dining-halls were two in number, one for the men and women and one for the children. The women ate at two long tables, while one table was set aside for the men.

---

[1] John Swainson, in his article on the Colony of Bishop Hill in the January number of *Scandinavia*, 1885.

The tables were covered with linen table-cloths, which were changed three times a week. The table service was neat, durable and substantial. Twelve waitresses served at the tables, while eighteen persons were employed in the kitchen as cooks or in other capacities. Soup was boiled in a monster kettle holding from forty to fifty gallons, and everything in the unitary cuisine was arranged on a similarly magnificent scale. The food was wholesome and substantial. No luxuries were indulged in; pastry of every description was banished, except on the great church holidays and on the Fourth of July. The abundance which prevailed was quite a contrast from the poverty of early days, when the community had been frequently obliged to observe fast-days for want of food, and when only one meal had been forthcoming on Sundays. A beef and several hogs were butchered each week. Mush and pure milk were extensively used. The bread was made of pumpkin meal and wheat flour. The beverage consisted of coffee and small beer. Nothing was allowed to go to waste, and it was estimated that the cost of board per person was about three cents a day.

Clothing was correspondingly cheap, for the society manufactured its own linen, flannel, jean and dress goods. The women cut and sewed their own clothes, while the men's suits were made at the society's tailor shop. The society dressed its own leather and made its own shoes. Every person received each year two suits of clothes, together with one pair of boots and one of shoes. On work-days the women wore blue drilling, but on holidays they appeared in calico and gingham. The men dressed either in jeans or in woolen stuffs, and wore their hair long. The society adopted no fixed styles, but nevertheless a certain uniformity of dress prevailed.

With regard to the institution of the family, its relations, at first, remained intact. Whole families occupied one-room tenements. Single persons dwelt together in separate quarters according to sex. With the exception of the modifications imposed by the unitary cuisine, the home-life of the Jansonists differed in nowise materially from that of their neighbors under the individualistic system. But a change also in this respect was impending.

Of the twelve apostles appointed by Eric Janson to convert the world, Nils Heden alone had met with any degree of success. Besides making a number of converts, he visited several of the principal religious communistic settlements in the United States. From Hopedale, N. Y., he persuaded twenty-five or thirty persons to join the Bishop Hill Colony. He also established friendly relations with the Oneida Perfectionists of New York and the Rappists of Pennsylvania. In 1854 he made a journey to Pleasant Hill, Kentucky, which was destined to have important consequences.

The Shakers taught the Jansonists the advantages of raising small fruit, and instructed them in improved methods of dyeing wool. From Pleasant Hill also the Jansonists got improved breeds of cattle. A number of the Jansonists accepted Shakerism and went to live at Pleasant Hill, among them being the widow of Eric Janson.

On his visit in 1854, Nils Heden allowed himself to be converted to the doctrine of celibacy. Returning to Bishop Hill he won the support of Jonas Olson, who straightway proceeded to ingraft the new doctrine upon the Jansonist creed. The practice of celibacy was somewhat difficult of enforcement. Some of the members of the community objected strenuously, but they were dealt with according to article 3 of the by-laws, which provided that any person guilty of preaching and disseminating religious doctrines contrary to those of the Bible might be expelled. Thus, after a number of voluntary resignations and forcible expulsions, the opposition was broken and submission secured.

After the introduction of celibacy the families continued to live together as heretofore, only that married persons were enjoined to practice restraint in the conjugal relations, and new marriages were, of course, prohibited. Under such circumstances celibacy could not be strictly enforced, and remained a constant source of irritation, becoming eventually a potent factor in hastening the dissolution of the community.

The Jansonists placed great value upon elementary education. Ever since the winter of 1847–8 the community had kept an English day-school, employing usually a native American as principal, and appointing one or more of its own members as assistant teachers. At one time, as stated above, the society was joined by a number of American communistic families from Hopedale, N. Y., among whom were several persons competent to teach. These families did not remain long, however, and the society was again compelled to resort to outside help.

At first the school was conducted in mud-caves or any vacant room, but later a fine brick school-house, with accommodations for several hundred pupils, was erected. The average attendance was about one hundred, the school age being limited to fourteen years. The number of school months in the year was six. Swedish was not taught in the school, and the only knowledge which the children obtained of the language was through their parents. On the whole, the Jansonists evinced a commendable zeal in acquiring and adopting the language and customs of the country. Thus, for instance, the records of the Bishop Hill Colony were kept in the English as well as in the Swedish language.

When the school days were over there were no means of continuing the studies. With the exception of the Bible, the Jansonists had destroyed all their books before leaving Sweden. Newspapers were not allowed. So there was no reading matter to be had except the Bible, the Jansonist hymn-book and catechism, and the well-worn school-books. Individuals sometimes happened upon other reading matter. Strangers stopping at the hotel occasionally left newspapers and books, which were surreptitiously circulated among the youthful members of the community. Among those who in this manner kept alive their appetite for knowledge were men since famous in letters and politics.

The church organization was loose. There was no regularly ordained clergy. Any one with the gift of expression might preach. But the general management of ecclesiastical affairs was intrusted to Jonas Olson, assisted by Olof Stenberg, Andreas Berglund, Nils Heden and Olof Aasberg. Under Jonas Olson's leadership the religious tendency was, in some respects, one of conservative retrogression. He modified some of the excesses of the Jansonist theology in a Devotionalistic direction, abolishing the Jansonist catechism altogether and thoroughly revising the hymn-book in 1857.

Thus, it will be seen, community life at Bishop Hill had its lights and its shadows. Which predominated it is impossible at this distance to say. In order to judge correctly, one must be able to comprehend the dominant motives of action. These were of a religious nature. They decided the complexion of the social and economic life. But they did not determine the intrinsic merits or demerits of the communistic system. All reasonable material wants, at any rate, were abundantly satisfied. No one was obliged to overtax his strength. Each one was put to the work for which he was best adapted. The aged and the infirm were cared for. The children were educated. Everybody was secure in the knowledge that, whatever befall, his subsistence was a certainty. On the whole, the members of the community enjoyed a greater amount of comfort and security against want than the struggling pioneer settlers by whom they were surrounded.

VII.—Disastrous Financial Speculations, Internal Dissensions, and Dissolution of the Society.

One of the grandest elements in the early development of the State of Illinois was the Illinois and Michigan Canal, connecting the Illinois and Mississippi rivers with the Great Lakes. The canal was recommended by Governor Bond in his first message to the State Legislature. In 1821 an appropriation of ten thousand dollars was made for the purpose of surveying the route. The estimated cost of the canal was from $600,000 to $700,000. The actual cost was $8,000,000.

Pending the construction of the canal, speculation in land broke out in 1834 and 1835. From Chicago the disease spread over the State. In 1834 and 1837 it seized upon the State Legislature, which forthwith enacted a system of internal improvements without parallel in grandeur of conception. It ordered the construction of 1300 miles of railway, although the population of the State was not 400,000. The railroad projects were surpassed by the schemes for the building of canals and the improvement of rivers. There were few counties that were not touched by railroad, river or canal, and those that were not were to be compensated by the free distribution among them of $200,000. The work was to commence simultaneously upon all river crossings, and at both ends of all railroads and rivers. The appropriations were $12,000,000, commissioners being appointed to borrow money on the credit of the State.

About this time the State Bank was loaning its funds freely to Godfrey, Gilman & Co., and other houses, for the purpose of diverting trade from St. Louis to Alton. These houses failed and took down the bank with them. In 1840 the State was loaded with a debt of $14,000,000. There was not a dollar in the treasury, credit was gone, and the good money in circulation was not sufficient to pay the interest for a single year.

But in 1848 the Illinois and Michigan Canal was finally completed, and began turning into the treasury an annual net sum of $111,000. The industries of the State revived, and the projects for the internal development of the country were again brought forward, with the difference, however, that they were now supported by private instead of public enterprise.

In 1854 the managers of the Chicago, Burlington and

Quincy Railroad proposed to run their line into Bishop Hill. But the Jansonists, apprehensive of the probable effects of the intrusion, objected, and the railroad instead went through Galva, five miles distant. This did not prevent the Jansonists from entering upon a $37,000 contract with the company to grade a portion of the roadbed.

The manner in which Galva was founded is so illustrative of the origin of most Western towns and of the practices of railway corporations in general, that the following quotation from Kett's History of Henry County is inserted in full: "The idea of building a town upon this site was first entertained in 1853. While Messrs. J. M. & Wm. L. Wiley were traveling from Peoria County to Rock Island in the spring of that year, they were attracted by the beauty of the surrounding country, and halted their team on the ground that now forms College Park, across which the old trail led. Standing in their buggy and looking out upon the scene, one of them remarked to the other, 'Let us buy the land and lay out a town!' At this time there were only two or three buildings to be seen from that point, and the country around was one vast sea of prairie, over which the deer were still roaming at will. The land was shortly purchased by them, and after negotiating with the C. B. & Q. Railroad Company a full year, they finally secured the location of a depot upon their purchase by donating the land now owned and occupied by the company in the center of the town. In the fall of the year succeeding its purchase (1854), and about the time that the arrangement with the railroad company was effected, the town was laid out in its present shape by the gentlemen mentioned. The cars commenced running in December of the same year."[1]

On account of its location on the railroad, Galva could not fail to become an object of interest to the Bishop Hill Colony. The community purchased fifty town lots, and lent its money

[1] History of Henry County, published by H. J. Kett & Co., Chicago, pp. 168–9.

and influence towards building up the place. The station was named after the populous seaboard town of Gefle in the province of Helsingland, Sweden, although the name was soon corrupted to Galva. The Jansonists built the first house and dug the first well. Before the close of 1855 the society had erected a hotel, a general store, and a large brick warehouse, the material for which was hauled from Bishop Hill.

The Bishop Hill Colony was represented in these business enterprises by Olof Johnson, a member of the Board of Trustees. Olof Johnson was originally a peasant from Söderala Parish, So. Helsingland. He was one of the leaders appointed by Eric Janson to conduct the Jansonist emigration. Later he had been sent by Eric Janson on a business trip to Sweden. Upon the adoption of the charter he was as a matter of course given a position as trustee. When Galva became the business headquarters of Bishop Hill he was appointed by the trustees to represent them in that place. As the business in Galva increased in volume and importance it was natural that the business in Bishop Hill should also fall under his control. In so far as his plans met with Jonas Olson's approval he dictated the business policy of the community. The two supplemented each other, Jonas Olson managing the internal affairs of the community, while Olof Johnson managed its external affairs. Olof Johnson made Galva his headquarters, but otherwise spent much of his time in New York, Philadelphia, Boston, Chicago, St. Louis, New Orleans, Mobile, and other points where the community transacted business. He was of a hearty, social disposition, and was a universal favorite wherever he went. He was not educated, being unable even to keep his own accounts, but possessed, it was thought, great natural talent for business.

The society was now excellently organized for the purposes of economic production. The several departments of industry were under the charge of superintendents who were responsible to the Board of Trustees. Under the superintendents were the foremen of gangs of workmen. According to a later arrangement the trustees were expected to meet every Monday evening for the consideration of the affairs of the community, and on the first Monday of every month any member might consult with the trustees on matters of general importance.

The first report of the trustees was made on January 21, 1855. According to this report the society owned 8028 acres of land, improved and unimproved, fifty town lots in Galva, improved and unimproved, valued at ten thousand dollars, also ten shares in the Central Military Track Railroad valued at one thousand dollars, together with five hundred and eighty-six head of cattle, one hundred and nine horses and mules, one thousand hogs, and divers poultry, unthreshed wheat, flax, broom-corn, etc. Furthermore, the community possessed other property to the value of $37,471.02. The entire debt amounted to only $18,000. Some idea of the effectiveness of the industrial organization may be obtained from the fact that the subsequent reports show an average annual increase in personal property alone of $44,042.96.

Meanwhile Olof Johnson was developing a brilliant, if not altogether sound business policy. He managed to make his influence paramount in the Board of Trustees, obtaining control over four of the seven votes. This made him to a certain extent independent of Jonas Olson's dictation, although the latter could by his influence with the people have prevented any scheme distasteful to him from being realized. The very fact that Jonas Olson did not choose to exercise this influence, even when he disagreed most with Olof Johnson, makes him morally responsible for the latter's disastrous financial mistakes.

Olof Johnson's idea was to make the community rich by employing its resources to build up manufactories and establish a large general business. Jonas Olson's policy, on the other hand, was distinctively an agricultural policy. At first Olof Johnson was eminently successful. Prices went up during the Crimean war. Wheat went up from thirty-five cents to one dollar and fifty cents a bushel. Broom-corn rose from fifty dollars to a hundred and fifty dollars a ton. Oats and Indian corn advanced correspondingly. The steam flour mill at Bishop Hill was kept running night and day, turning out a hundred barrels of flour every twenty-four hours. Olof Johnson erected at Galva a pork-packing establishment and an elevator for the storage of grain. He operated a coal mine, dealt in stocks and bonds, and purchased real estate, holding at one time one hundred and sixty acres of land within the present limits of Chicago. In 1856, together with Robert C. Schenk, sometime U. S. Minister to England, and other prominent men, he planned the construction of the Western Air Line Railroad, which was to run from Fort Wayne, Indiana, through to Iowa. He made a five million dollar contract with the company to grade the roadbed from Indiana to the Mississippi, accepting one million dollars in bonds as part payment. In the same year he entered into the banking business, becoming secretary of the Nebraska Western Exchange Bank in Galva.

But after the Crimean war came the financial crisis of 1857. Illinois lost two hundred and fifty banks at one fell swoop. One of the first to go was the classic Bank of Oxford, located in the hazel-brush near Bishop Hill, and the Nebraska Western Exchange Bank soon followed. The Western Air Line Railroad shared the fate of the banks, and left the Jansonists a worthless debt of thirty-four thousand dollars for actual work performed.

The inevitable reaction against the management of the trustees set in. The people began to accuse them, and especially Olof Johnson, of transcending their powers and squandering the property of the community. The most wonderful stories were circulated concerning the extravagance of Olof Johnson. He was reported to have gambled away, in New York, a fortune in a single night. In Chicago he was said to have bribed the police with fabulous sums when they broke in upon his midnight orgies. In St. Louis, so it was rumored, he bought a steamboat to amuse his friends for a single night, and in New Orleans, in company of Southern slave-owners, he was claimed to have lit his imported cigars with bank-notes, boasting of his white slaves in Bishop Hill who needed no bloodhounds or whipping-posts to keep them to their task.

Following the flush times preceding 1857 came a complete or partial standstill in nearly all lines of industry. The members of the community were no longer deceived and quieted by a great show of business. The disaffection which was brewing took form in 1857 in an attempt to secure the repeal of the charter. The attempt was frustrated by the judicious expenditure on the part of Olof Johnson of six thousand dollars in Springfield. But in 1858 and 1859 resolutions were passed at the annual meeting looking to the control of the actions of the Board of Trustees by the society.

On January 9, 1860, the treasurer of the community read the following annual statement of the Board of Trustees:

ASSETS.

Farm lands	$414,824	00
Galva real estate	33,228	47
Buildings and improvements	129,508	61
Horses and mules	21,520	00
Cattle account	17,088	00
Hog account	1,700	00
Sheep account	1,400	00
Poultry	50	00
Implements, farming	5,965	00
Furniture and movables	11,610	14
Steam mills	1,454	70
Boarding-house utensils	3,096	40
Mechanical department	9,092	88
Produce	4,616	00
Merchandise	4,775	60

County bonds	$56,000 00
Railroad stock	21,765 78
Western Exchange Bank stock	9,500 00
Bills receivable	46,144 45
Due from N. A. L. R. R. Co	33,826 91
Due from the estate of Radcliffe	3,907 48
Due from Stark County	6,000 00
Personal account	8,521 91
Cash	581 25
	$846,277 58

LIABILITIES.

Bills payable	74,014 56
Personal account	1,630 78
Balance	770,631 94
	$846,277 58
Balance stock on hand	$770,630 94

The accuracy of this statement was questioned and a committee was appointed to make a thorough examination of the community's books, the trustees asking for a delay of three weeks, which was granted.

Pending the examination of the books, special meetings were held by the members of the community, at which a new set of by-laws, calculated to restrict the powers of the trustees, was adopted. The preamble explains sufficiently the temper of the by-laws: "Whereas, the members of the Bishop Hill Colony have each one carefully considered and reflected upon the situation and condition of the general affairs of the Colony and the intention of its organization; and, Whereas, the general conviction has been acknowledged and expressed that the design and end for which this Colony was established never can be obtained under the present system of management; and, Whereas, the necessity requires and demands a change and reform in conducting and managing the affairs and property of the Colony: Therefore, to effect this just and needful change, the Bishop Hill Colony has this day adopted the following by-laws."

The principal provisions of the new by-laws were as follows: The trustees might not buy or sell real estate, nor make contracts and debts binding upon the community, without the latter's express permission. The trustees were to be guided in other matters by the general instructions of the community. The general business meetings were to be held monthly instead of annually. The main office of the trustees should be in Bishop Hill and not in Galva. In case of withdrawal, members were to be entitled to fixed compensation for the property and labor which they had contributed to the society.[1] The trustees, however, refused to acknowledge the legality of the meetings in which the by-laws had been adopted. As they persistently declined to appear in the monthly meetings, or to render any account whatever of their management, a resolution was passed, in which they were declared to have forfeited the confidence of the community and were requested to hand in their resignations. The resolution failed of its object.

In October, 1860, Olof Johnson, as the principal offender, was formally deposed from office. But he secured an injunction against the Bishop Hill Colony, and had himself, together with certain of his friends, appointed receivers to wind up the affairs of the corporation. For on February 14, 1860, a plan had been agreed upon looking to the dissolution of the society and the allotment in severalty of the communal property. This plan provided for a preliminary extra-legal division of property between the Olson and the Johnson parties, the former receiving two hundred and sixty-five shares out of a total of four hundred and fifteen. By being appointed a receiver for the Bishop Hill Colony, Olof Johnson got control, not only of the shares belonging to his own, but also of those belonging to the opposite party.

---

[1] For complete text see Appendix.

On May 24, 1861, in order to prevent any inconveniences which might arise from the infringement of legal technicalities and to facilitate the final individualization of the property, Olof Johnson was not only reinstated as a trustee, but was also invested with powers of attorney to settle with the creditors of the community. Property more than sufficient to extinguish all claims against the society was set aside for that purpose, and the trustees were given five years in which to accomplish the work, an annual report of progress being required.

In the spring of 1861 the Johnson party perfected the individualization of its property, each member entering upon the complete possession of his share. The distribution was made on the following basis: To every person, male and female, that had attained the age of thirty-five years, a full share of all lands, timber, town lots, and personal property was given. A full share consisted of twenty-two acres of land, one timber lot—nearly two acres—one town lot, and an equal part of all barns, horses, cattle, hogs, sheep, or other domestic animals, and all farming implements and household utensils. All under this age received a share corresponding in amount and value to the age of the individual, no discrimination being shown to either sex. The smallest share was about eight acres of land, a correspondingly small town lot and timber lot, and part of the personal property. Thus a man over thirty-five years of age, having a wife of that age or over, would receive considerable property to manage. He held that of his wife and children in trust, the deeds being made in the name of the head of the family.

In the spring of the following year the Olson party followed suit, so that after March, 1862, the Bishop Hill Colony was practically extinct. It is a singular fact that this division, comprising, among other property, no less than about twelve hundred acres of land, has always been regarded as thoroughly just, and it is believed no complaint has ever been raised against it.

The members of the community now considered that their financial troubles were at an end. But they were grievously mistaken. The trustees made no reports. On the contrary, in 1865, Olof Johnson assessed the individualized lands ten dollars an acre, which assessment, aside from the property already reserved by the trustees, was sufficiently large to pay the entire debt of the community. In 1868 an additional assessment of eleven dollars per acre was made. This was more than the members would stand, and on July 27, 1868, a committee was appointed to bring suit by bill in chancery against the trustees. In this suit, the special master in chancery, in referring to the trustees' financial statement of January 9, 1860, said: "Upon the making of said report . . . the Colony, at the same meeting where the said report was made, appointed a committee to examine and revise all the accounts of the Colony for the past year and make report. After the appointment of the committee and before they were given access to the Colony books for examination, new books were made up under the direction of some of the trustees, and these new books, instead of the original, were shown to the said committee for their examination. The difference between the new and original books is the said sum of $42,759.33. Upon my order to the said trustees to produce the Colony books, the said new books, and not the original, were produced." The special master found that, at the date of his report, Olof Johnson and the trustees were indebted to the Bishop Hill Colony in the sum of $109,619.29.

It is not the intention to rehearse the details of this tedious and expensive lawsuit. Some of the principals are still living. The suit impoverished many, and destroyed much of the harmony and good-will which still existed at the dissolution of the society. The "Colony Case" lasted twelve years, and was famous in its day among the legal fraternity in Illinois. After the death of Olof Johnson, in 1870, it languished until, in 1879, it was ended on the basis of a compromise.

VIII.—Conclusion.

In concluding this monograph upon the history of the Bishop Hill Colony, it will be profitable to inquire what were the principal advantages of the communistic system, and what were the principal causes of its failure.

One immediate cause of failure was, of course, the disastrous financial management for which the Board of Trustees, and especially Olof Johnson, were responsible. The defects of the charter and first set of by-laws, which hardly left the community a supervisory control in the management of its own affairs, have been reviewed. Under the circumstances it was not surprising that the trustees, well-intentioned as they undoubtedly were, should be tempted to exercise their powers to further arbitrary schemes of aggrandizement. This temptation was increased by the speculative temper of the general business world in the flush times preceding 1857.

A second cause of failure was the religious tyranny exercised by the Board of Trustees, and especially by Jonas Olson. This tyranny culminated in the arbitrary introduction of celibacy, in the accomplishment of which drastic measures were freely resorted to. In 1859, religious dissensions ran so high that all community of worship was apparently destroyed. A strong reformatory party, led by Nils Heden, demanded and obtained important concessions from the Board of Trustees, which, however, led to no permanent conciliatory results.

A third cause was the importation of ideas and habits of thought antagonistic to the communal life. This was due to the building of railroads, and to improved means of communication generally with the outside world. Even under ordinary circumstances the transferring of interests from one generation to another is a delicate and painful process. Under the peculiar circumstances which obtained in Bishop Hill, it was perhaps impossible of accomplishment. The communism of the Jansonists was founded upon a religious basis. As soon as this basis should be withdrawn, the superstructure was destined to fall. And that is what happened, for with the death of its founder, Jansonism rapidly went into decay. At the best there was little attraction in the religious life in Bishop Hill.

The advantages of the system were such as were derived either from the application of the collectivist principle in the process of production, or from an equal distribution of economic goods. Labor was saved, consumption of every description was reduced, starvation was impossible. Yet, while the Jansonists fared well materially, and while it is true they laid stress upon elementary education, the general intellectual life was exceedingly restricted. But perhaps it was not any more so than that of the back-woodsmen by whom they were surrounded. One thing is certain, the Jansonists displayed a wonderful amount of skill and ingenuity in all trades and mechanical arts.

When the allotment in severalty took place, the majority of the Jansonists left Bishop Hill and moved out upon their farm lands. The division took place in a fortunate period. During the War of Secession, high prices were obtained for agricultural produce, and the more thrifty and fortunate were enabled to accumulate handsome competences.

Of the persons who have figured in the foregoing pages the majority are now dead. John Root was sentenced to imprisonment for two years in the State penitentiary. He died some years after his release, friendless and penniless, in Chicago. Mrs. Eric Janson, once so handsome and gifted and powerful, ended her days in the County Poor House in 1888, and lies buried in the community's burying-ground at Bishop Hill. Eric Janson, Jr., grew to manhood in Bishop Hill, and is now a successful newspaper editor in Holdrege, Nebraska. Jonas Olson still preaches occasionally in the Old Colony Church, and although his voice trembles and his frame shakes, the fire of the old-time eloquence is not wholly wanting. It is well that his eyes are growing dim, for the congregation which greets him is becoming piteously small, and looks grotesquely out of place in such a pretentious house of worship. The majority of the Jansonists have joined the Methodist communion, and even Jonas Olson no longer adheres to the old faith, but is now an independent Second Day Adventist.

The present town of Bishop Hill numbers only three hundred and thirty-three inhabitants. The shops and the mills and the manufactories are empty, and the very dwelling-houses are going to ruin. In the light of the past, it is truly a Deserted Village. But the spruce and the elm and the black walnut saplings that were planted in the days of the Colony have grown into magnificent shade trees, and speak of the glory of the past.

APPENDIX.

The Charter of the Bishop Hill Colony.

An Act incorporating the Bishop Hill Colony at Bishop Hill, in Henry County.

Section 1. Be it enacted by the people of the State of Illinois, represented in General Assembly, that Olof Johnson, John[1] Olson, James Ericson, Jacob Jacobson, Jonas Kronberg, Swan Swanson, Peter Johnson, and their associates and successors be, and they are hereby constituted and appointed, a body politic and corporate, by the name and style of "The Bishop Hill Colony," and by that name they and their successors shall and may have perpetual succession, shall be capable of suing and being sued, defending and being defended, pleading and being impleaded, answering and being answered, within all courts and places whatsoever, and they may have a common seal, to alter or change the same at pleasure; may purchase and hold or convey real and personal property necessary to promote and fully carry out the objects of said corporation.

The number of Trustees shall be seven, and the above-named persons are hereby appointed and constituted Trustees of said corporation.

Section 2. The real and personal estate held and owned by said Trustees, in their corporate capacity, shall be held and used for the benefit, support, and profit of the members of the Colony.

Section 3. The business of said corporation shall be manufacturing, milling, all kinds of mechanical business, agriculture and merchandising.

---

[1] Anglicized for Jonas.

Section 4. The said Trustees, above appointed, shall hold their office during good behavior, but are liable to be removed, for good reason, by a majority of the male members of said Colony.

Section 5. All vacancies in the office of Trustees, either by removal, death, resignation, or otherwise, shall be filled in such manner as shall be provided by the by-laws of such corporation.

Section 6. The said Trustees and their successors in office may make contracts, purchase real estate, and again convey the same, whenever they shall see proper so to do, for the benefit of the Colony.

Section 7. All the real estate heretofore conveyed by any person or persons to the Trustees of the Bishop Hill Society, shall be, and the titles to said lands are hereby invested in the said Trustees above appointed, for the uses and purposes above specified.

Section 8. The said Bishop Hill Colony may pass such by-laws concerning the government and management of the property and business of said Colony, and the admission, withdrawal and expulsion of its members, and regulating its internal policy and for other purposes, directly connected with the business and management of said Colony, as they may deem proper, not inconsistent with the Constitution and by-laws of the State.

Section 9. This act shall be deemed and taken as a public act, and shall be construed liberally for the benefit of said Colony.

The Old By-Laws of the Bishop Hill Colony.

Article 1. Any person sustaining a good moral character may become a member of this Colony by transferring to the trustees thereof all his or her real and personal property, and subscribing to these by-laws. The Board of Trustees shall determine the question of moral character and admission, and a majority of said trustees shall constitute a quorum for that purpose. The trustees may, in their discretion, refer the question of admission to a vote of the adult male members of the Colony.

ARTICLE 2. The property which any person on becoming a member of this Colony shall transfer to the trustees thereof, shall become forever thereafter the absolute property of the Colony; and on withdrawal or discontinuance of membership by any person, he shall not be entitled to compensation or pay for any services or labor he may have performed during the time he may have been a member; but it shall be at the option of the trustees to give to such person such things, whether money or property, as they, the trustees, shall deem right or proper.

ARTICLE 3. Any member who shall be guilty of disturbing the peace and harmony of this society, by vicious or wicked conduct, or by preaching and disseminating doctrines of a religious belief contrary to the doctrines of the Bible which are generally received and believed by this Colony, may be expelled.

ARTICLE 4. It shall be the duty of the trustees of said Colony to regulate and direct the various industrial pursuits and business of said Colony in person or by such agents or foremen as they may see fit to appoint from time to time, and to require such agents or foremen to account to them in such manner and at such time as they, the trustees, shall deem convenient and proper.

ARTICLE 5. There shall be held annually, on the second Monday of January in each year, a meeting of the adult male members of said Colony for the general transaction of business, at which time the Board of Trustees shall make a full and complete report of the financial condition and affairs of the Colony for the year ending on the Saturday next previous to such meeting. But the Board of Trustees, or a majority of them, may call special meetings of the adult male members of the Colony for the consideration and transaction of business, whenever in their opinion the interests of the Colony require it. And a special meeting shall convene whenever a majority of the male adult members of the Colony shall require such meeting, by signifying their request to the trustees in writing five days previous to such meeting.

ARTICLE 6. Our property and industry and the proceeds thereof shall constitute a common fund, from, by and with which it shall be the duty of the Board of Trustees to provide for the subsistence, comfort and reasonable wants of every member of the Colony, for the support of the aged and infirm, for the care and cure of the sick and the burial of the dead, and for the proper education of our children, and generally to do and transact any and all business necessary to the prosperity, happiness and usefulness of the Colony, and consistent with the charter organizing the same.

ARTICLE 7. Whenever a vacancy shall occur in the Board of Trustees, the same shall be filled at an election held for that purpose by the adult male members of the Colony, and the person receiving the highest number of votes shall be trustee.

ARTICLE 8. These by-laws may be revised, altered or amended at any regular or called meeting of the adult male members of the Colony, by a majority of those present and voting at such meeting.

THE NEW BY-LAWS OF THE BISHOP HILL COLONY.

ARTICLE 1. All heretofore adopted by-laws, orders, decisions and commissions, either to the trustees, or issued by the trustees to any of them, or to other persons belonging or not belonging to the Colony, that have heretofore been in force, are hereby, to all power and value, repealed.

ARTICLE 2. All persons who according to the former by-laws have become members of this Colony and are now residing within this Colony, shall be members under these by-laws, and be entitled to all the rights and benefits that these by-laws prescribe.

ARTICLE 3. In accordance with the charter dated January 17, A. D. 1853, organizing this Colony, the trustees may buy and sell real and personal property and make contracts; but in conformity with the 1st and 8th sections of said charter, the Colony does hereby decree that the trustees shall not buy or sell real estate or make contracts, or contract debts for which the Colony shall be holden, unless the Colony has in a general meeting been heard and has decided on all the stipulations in regard to such purchases, sale, contracts or indebtedness, as the Colony may consider best to carry out the intention of its organization.

ARTICLE 4. The trustees shall carefully regulate the affairs, works, and industrial pursuits of the Colony; make purchases, sales, and conduct the finances in accordance with such ordinances and instructions as the Colony may, in general meeting, from time to time adopt and issue.

ARTICLE 5. Foremen of shops, mechanical establishments, and agricultural departments shall be chosen by the Colony, and such foremen shall account to the trustees at such time and in such manner as the trustees may direct for the business that such foremen may execute.

ARTICLE 6. The Colony may adopt such rules of order as necessity may require to promote morality, decency, justice and equity between the members.

ARTICLE 7. On the second Monday in each month, at 9 o'clock A. M., there shall be a general meeting of the adult male members of the Colony, for the transaction of the general business of the Colony. All motions introduced at such meetings shall be put to vote, and the motion shall be decided according to the will of the majority, as expressed by the vote. These votings shall, if not otherwise decided, be made in such manner that the names of the members shall be called, whereupon each member shall respond to the call of his name with "aye" or "no," and shall thereby signify whether he is voting for or against the motion; "aye" signifying approbation of the motion, and "no" signifying disapprobation of the same. At these meetings the trustees shall render and deliver a report and full account of the affairs of the Colony and the management of the same for the month ending next before such meeting, and also a summary account of the affairs of the Colony up to the time of that meeting at which such account is rendered.

ARTICLE 8. The Colony may, whenever it shall so decide, elect five men, who shall constitute a committee for an examination, investigation, and inspection of the reports, accounts and transactions of the trustees; and it shall be the duty of the trustees to deliver to the said investigating committee such documents as said committee may call for for such examination, investigation and inspection; and the trustees shall also give such information and explanation as the said committee may see proper to demand. The investigation ordered at the general meeting of the 9th of January, A. D. 1859, shall proceed according to the instructions, or in the manner that may be hereafter directed.

ARTICLE 9. Should a vacancy occur in the Board of Trustees, either by death, resignation, removal or discharge, such vacancy shall be filled at a general meeting by a vote of the male members of the Colony, and the person who shall receive the highest number of votes shall be trustee.

ARTICLE 10. The affairs and transactions of the Colony shall be done in the name of the Colony. The trustees and the other officers shall have a common office at Bishop Hill, but at no other place, where the affairs shall be transacted and recorded.

ARTICLE 11. The income of the Colony shall be used for the support, clothing and subsistence of the members of the Colony and their families, for the education of their children, medical aid and care of the sick, and the funeral expenses of the dead; and all these expenses shall be paid from the common funds, and the surplus, after the debts of the Colony are liquidated, shall be used as the Colony may prescribe.

ARTICLE 12. Should any of the members wish to leave,

withdraw, and discontinue their membership in the Colony, they shall signify their intention at a general meeting, or before one of the trustees of the Colony; and such withdrawing or discontinuing member shall be entitled to compensation for the work he or she may have performed for the Colony; which compensation shall be computed and paid in such a manner that each and every person now residing in the Colony who is a member thereof, or has resided in the Colony for the last five years with the intention and promise to become a member of the Colony, shall be entitled to an equal amount of money for every six months he or she resides at Bishop Hill or in the Colony, after the time he or she has attained the age of eighteen years; which amount of money shall be fixed and calculated after the value of the real and personal estate belonging to the Colony, with deductions of the liabilities, in such a manner that all the separate amounts put together shall make the net balance of the value of the real and personal property of the Colony, according to the valuation of the property. And any person who signifies his or her intention to leave or withdraw from the membership shall receive the compensation for the work in the Colony according to such calculations, but such person's membership shall not cease before the said compensation has been respectively paid over to the proper person.

To find out the right value of the real and personal property, that the amount of compensation can with certainty be calculated and computed, the Colony shall appoint two disinterested and skillful persons, and these two persons shall select a third person who shall make a complete inventory and a true valuation of the real and personal property of the Colony, which inventory and valuation shall be completed before the first of June next: before this time, or the first of June next, the Trustees shall make a true statement of all the liabilities and claims of or on the Colony, and the net balance of the assets shall be the amount according to which the compensation, as has heretofore been stated, shall be computed and paid. The payment of said compensation for work to such persons as withdraw from the membership of the Colony shall be made in real and personal property, if mutual agreement can be made in regard to the situation of the real estate and the nature and quality of the personal property, and when such an agreement can be made, then shall the property be taken for the value that has been set on the same, as mentioned in this article, and the payment of such compensation shall be made within six months from the date when the person made the notification of his or her withdrawal.

ARTICLE 13. These by-laws can be altered or amended at a general meeting of the adult male members of the colony, with the exception of the 12th article of these by-laws, which cannot be repealed or amended; otherwise than that a yearly valuation of real and personal property can be made, if the Colony so decide.

ERIC JANSON

AND THE

BISHOP HILL COLONY

By

SIVERT ERDAHL

Reprinted from the Journal of the Illinois State Historical Society, vol. xviii, No. 3 (October, 1925)

CONTENTS.

Part I.

INTRODUCTORY.

9. The conversation Sunday evening and the reproach of the visitor.
10. The part which the visitor was henceforth to play in Sweden.

II.

Personal History of Eric Janson Until the Beginning of His Career As Religious Leader.

1. His parents.
2. His early childhood.
3. His condition after the confirmation age.
4. His conversion.
5. His first preaching.
6. The period when he did not preach.
7. His marriage and the subsequent six years.
8. His second beginning as a preacher.
9. His preaching in his home locality.

III.

Eric Janson's Career As Religious Leader In Sweden.

1. Personal characteristics.
2. More about his first visit to Helsingland.
3. His characteristics as a preacher.
4. His "vision."
5. His attempts at miraculous healing.
6. His fourth visit to Helsingland, and his moving thither.
7. The forming of a separate party.

Part III.

THE BISHOP HILL COLONY.

I.

The Colony During Janson's Rule.

II.

The Colony After Janson's Death.

1. Janson's successor.
2. The return of Jonas Olson and the beginning of a new regime.
3. Incorporation of the colony.
4. New prosperity.
5. A paragraph from "The Practical Christian."
6. The communist of the Jansonists.
7. Impressions of a visitor in 1853.
8. Preaching and education.
9. Arrogance in some of the leaders.
10. Introduction of celibacy.
11. The misery brought about through this doctrine.
12. Unhappy speculations.
13. Discontent of the young people.
14. The dissolution of communism.
15. Further financial troubles.
16. The Jansonists in the Civil War.
17. The colony in the seventies.

Part IV.

CONCLUDING REMARKS.

ERIC JANSON AND THE BISHOP HILL COLONY.

By SIVERT ERDAHL.

PART ONE: INTRODUCTORY.

Traditionally, America has always been a refuge for all oppressed. For reasons political, social, economic, and religious, men from every civilized country have sought in the United States new homes and new opportunities. Thousands of them have come singly, or with their families; but others have come in groups. The Pilgrim Fathers were such, and such were the Harmonists, the Separatists of Zoar, Robert Owen and his communists, the Icarians, the members of the Amana Community. Such also were the Jansonists, the men who built Bishop Hill Colony.[1]

These men who came in groups usually sent one or more of their members in advance to make the necessary preparations for the intended settlement. So also did the leader of the Jansonists. In the latter part of 1845 there came to New York a man from Sweden to seek out in the New World a suitable place for the founding of a colony. The man's name was Olof Olson, and he was one of the prominent members known in Sweden as the Eric-Jansonists. He brought his wife with him and two of his children and also a few other persons. In New York he met O. G. Hedstrom, a fellow-countryman who had been converted to Methodism, and who was now preaching to the Scandinavian seamen in that city. This Hedstrom is the founder of the Swedish Methodist Church in America.[2] Mr. Hedstrom used a dismantled ship for a church, and in this ship rooms were set in order as a temporary dwelling for Olson and his family.[3] They remained there during the winter of 1845 and 46. Then they proceeded on their

[1] William Alfred Hinds: "American Communities," pp. 66, 92, 130, 268, 324.
[2] Eric Johnson and C. F. Peterson: "Svenskarne i Illinois," p. 27.
[3] M. A. Mikkelsen: "The Bishop Hill Colony," p. 26.

mission, and came to Victoria, Knox County, Illinois.[4] There they met Jonas Hedstrom, a brother of the New York pastor, a zealous preacher of Methodism. Olson now set out upon a prospective tour, seeking to find a locality suitable for the intended colony. He visited various parts in Illinois, and even made a tour into Wisconsin and Minnesota.[5] He was of the opinion that Illinois would best answer the purpose, and to this effect he wrote back to those in Sweden who had sent him. Before Olson had set out on his long errand across the ocean, there had come to Sweden favorable reports of the United States, the land of religious freedom and of opportunities, and these reports Olson now confirmed. On August 1st, 1846, sixty acres were bought in Olson's name near Red Oak Grove for $250 from the common fund of the Jansonists. Thus a beginning was made for the new colony.

At the time of Olson's arrival, Henry County, where the colony was to be founded, was less than ten years old, and it was only a little more than ten years since the first white man had settled in the locality. It was about eleven years since the first house was built, but a man had lived there previously in an old wagon. When the first election was held in the county, only fifty-eight votes were cast. The first church —a log structure—was only eight years old. It was only ten years since the first flour mill was built. There had been no lawyer in the county until the year previous to Olson's arrival.[6]

Eric Janson, the religious leader who had sent Olson, soon followed his advance agent. Before leaving Sweden, he had appointed four of his most prominent followers to be at the head of the intended mass emigration[7]. He himself with one companion had crossed the mountains of Norway on skis and had arrived in Christiana. There, it seems, he had awaited his wife and three children, with a few others, and with these had crossed over to Copenhagen and Hamburg,

[4] "Svenskarne i Illinois," p. 27.
[5] "The Bishop Hill Colony," p. 26.
[6] Eric Johnson and C. F. Peterson: "Svenskarne i Illinois," p. 18 fl.
[7] Ibid, p. 27.

and from there, by way of Hull and Liverpool, had arrived in New York.[8] It was in June, 1846, that he came with his little company to the great metropolis. From there he proceeded to Victoria, where, in the beginning of the following month, he again met Jonas Olson. In addition to the land purchased in Olson's name there were bought during this first year 156 acres in section 8 in the same township. As a site for the intended village there was selected Hoopal Grove, a tract in section 14, township 14, three miles distant from Red Oak Grove. Here in September Eric Janson himself bought 160 acres for $1.25 an acre, and on the same day were bought 320 acres from sections 23 and 24. The town site was beautifully located. There was a knoll, a spring, some oak groves, and a little stream, South Edward Creek. The colony was to receive the name of Bishop Hill, from Biskopskulla, the birthplace parish of the founder.[9]

And so was founded the Bishop Hill Colony. It was at once to become the most important settlement in Henry County. In four years it was to have more than one thousand members, a great deal more than one fourth of the population of the entire county. At its highest prosperity, the colony was to be the most important settlement between Peoria and Rock Island.[10] It was to reach such accomplishments that a writer[11] felt justified in saying later: "The diligence which this religious people exercised in their city of refuge, under the persecution of the world, influenced with epoch-making strength the general history of the county; and we do not exaggerate when we assert that the industrial activities which the colony carried on during its blossoming period have not been surpassed by any colony, founded on the same scale and under similar difficult circumstances, whether we keep ourselves to the confines of Henry County or go beyond." And the founding of the colony was to have effect

[8] Jonas Olson tells the story thus, according to Emil Herlenius: "Erik-Jansismens Historia," p. 60, note 2.

[9] Emil Herlenius: "Erik-Jansismens Historia," p. 63.

[10] M. A. Mikkelsen: "The Bishop Hill Colony," p. 5.

[11] Eric Johnson, the son of the founder, has thus expressed himself in "Svenskarne i Illinois," p. 21.

also in this respect: These early settlers broke the way for thousands of their fellow countrymen who came to build their homes in other parts of the United States.[12]

But the founder, in his dream, saw a much more wonderful vision. To him the colony was to be a New Jerusalem. Before leaving Sweden, he had pictured to his devoted followers how that, in the new land of promise, the glories of the Millennium should be theirs. They should have no difficulty with the new language; for among whatever strange people they should come there should be given them at once power to speak their tongue correctly. All should be as one great family. The lion should there eat straw like the ox. Serpents and scorpions should not harm the chosen people of God.[13] They should all have freedom unmolested to serve the Lord as they deemed right. And from this New Jerusalem should radiate the true Christianity which should convert America and from America should spread over all the world. Then should come the Millennium, and in this Millennium "Eric Janson, or the heirs of his body, should, as the representatives of Christ, reign to the end of all time."[14]

PART TWO: ERIC JANSON AND HIS ACTIVITIES IN SWEDEN.

I.

The Religious Condition of Sweden Prior to the Advent of Jansonism.

The condition of the Established Church in Sweden was, in the beginning of the nineteenth century, not the best imaginable. It was just emerging out of the darkness of the "Illumination Period." The "rationalism" characteristic of this period had dominated Europe during the previous cen-

[12] C. F. Petersen: "Ett Hundra Ar," p. 398.
[13] From Emil Herlenius: "Erik-Jansismens Historia," pp. 52 and 64.
[14] M. A. Mikkelsen: "The Bishop Hill Colony," pp. 25 and 26.

tury, and it had exerted its influence in Sweden also, though less there than in some other countries. Speaking about this period, Esaias Tegner said in a speech in 1817: "The foremost men of the times maintained, more or less explicitly, that all religion, and in particular our revealed religion, was a folk-tale serviceable for scaring children and keeping the mob under discipline, but for the rest unworthy of the era of light."[15] In 1810 or thereabout, the following appeared in a Swedish magazine: "We are to this extent orthodox in religion that we are perhaps regarded by the modern Christian naturalists as dangerous fanatics because we frankly dare to confess that we believe in the divinity of Christ and in the eternal necessity of the atonement and its existing power."[16] In the higher circles of society religious indifference or skepticism was the general thing. The young people, especially, deemed it an honor to be called "free-thinkers."[17] The Swedish king Gustaf III is reported to have said once that he could not lie so much in a year as the crown prince could in an hour when he, in child-like simplicity, gave account of his Christian faith.[18]

Although about 1810 a reaction against this illumination had set in, there was, nevertheless, during a decade on either side of 1825 a great deal of lifeless formalism in the land. To be sure, there were in the church pastors who were true shepherds, but perhaps the majority could not be thus designated. Their sermons were often laid out on such a high plane that the common people could understand little or nothing of what was said. Frequently, they were men who had little sympathy with the peasant's striving for salvation. Some were more interested in agriculture, in politics, and in all kinds of secular affairs of the community than they were in caring for the spiritual welfare of their parishioners.[19] They were liberal in their views on amusements. At wed-

[15] Quoted by C. A. Cornelius in his "Svenska Kyrkans Historia Efter Reformationen," vol. 2, p. 169.
[16] Ibid, p. 167.
[17] Quoted by C. A. Cornelius in his "Svenska Kyrkans Historia Efter Reformationen," vol. 2. p. 169.
[18] C. F. Petersen: "Ett Hundra Ar," p. 394.
[19] From Emil Herlenius: "Erik-Jansismens Historia," p. 2.

dings it was the standard custom that the pastor was to have the first dance with the bride. Of some pastors it could even be said that they did not live an outwardly irreproachable life. Not a few loved overmuch the glittering cup. At least one is known to have had a distillery, and the grain which the parishioners brought as their customary dues, he sold to them again in the form of liquor.[20] In short, worldliness characterized a great number of them. The light that should have shone was darkness.

In the shadow of this rationalistic, lifeless, form-bound Christianity were found some lay people, serious-minded men, who were deeply concerned about the salvation of their souls. They were in derision called "lasare"—literally, "readers." It is difficult to find a name which will convey to us the feeling which the word "lasare" conveyed to the people of Sweden. "Puritans" will not do, nor "pietists"; for neither is broad enough. Perhaps "Lollard" brought no more contempt in England than "lasare" in Sweden. For want of better words we will call them religionists or laymen. They were called "readers," not because they insisted upon reading the Bible only, as has been erroneously said, but because they evinced concern for spiritual things and because they read in seriousness both their Bible and other religious books. Chief among the latter were the works of Luther, Arndt, Thomas a Kempis, Muller, Scriver, Murbeck, Sellergren, Nohrborg, M. F. Ross, J. A. Hoffman.[21] They were opposed to card playing and dancing and other amusements commonly engaged in both by lay and learned. They gathered in their private houses to sing, to pray, to read the word of God, to comment upon it, and thus to edify each other. Some of them, it is true, went in upon roads that were not right, but they were, nevertheless, religionists, men concerned about the salvation of their souls and about the salvation of their unregenerated fellow men.

---

[20] See M. A. Mikkelsen: "The Bishop Hill Colony," p. 12.

[21] For this statement Herlenius refers to Ekendahl: "Bidrag till laseriets historia i Sverige," p. 14.

So much may be said about these religionists in a general way. But, as intimated, they were not all as one. In some parishes there were spiritually interested pastors who understood the longing for salvation which agitated some of the members of their congregations. Such pastors sought to help their troubled parishioners. They fashioned their sermons to the common man. They watched over the private religious gatherings of the religionists. They guided the Bible interpretations of the unschooled laymen, and spoke the word of God to them also outside of the regular Sunday service. Such pastors were appreciated, and people came to hear them even from neighboring parishes. In localities fortunate enough to have ministers of this type the religious awakening would often result in true conversions and in sincere, beautiful Christian lives. These people had been orthodox Lutherans in name before; now they were orthodox Lutherans in fact. They realized the truth of what Luther had said: "Faith is a living, busy, active, mighty thing, and it is impossible that it should not do good without ceasing; it does not ask whether good works ought to be done, but before the question is put, it has done them already, and is always engaged in doing them; you may as well separate burning and shining from fire, as works from faith."[22] These religionists did not form a sect. So far from separating from the church, they were the best members of the church. They were pietists in the best sense of the word. They were pilgrims fleeing from the City of Destruction, seeking an inheritance incorruptible, undefiled.

But some of the religionists entered upon devious paths. The laymen ranged all the way from orthodox Lutheran pietists to downright fanatics. The pastors were often blind to the religious needs of their parishioners; they were hirelings who left their flocks to shift for themselves, or even molested them. In localities having such ministers, the men who were troubled about their souls would be likely to receive

---

[22] As quoted by Philip Schaff: "History of the Christian Church," vol. 6, p. 22 fl.

no proper guidance. Expecting no spiritual assistance from their pastors, they often listened gladly to any one who talked religion. They also read religious books that were not of the most wholesome. Under such conditions nothing was more natural than that some should come to hold indefensible tenets and even drift into fanaticism. Some began to discourage the reading of all religious literature except the Bible and the writings of Luther.[23] Some developed an eccentric hatred for the Established Church which they considered completely permeated with worldliness. Some, claiming that the grace of God covered their sins, continued to sin in security. Some went to the other extreme and taught that even in this life a person could attain perfect purity of heart, perfect sinlessness. Some became melancholy; others excessively light-hearted. Some renounced various forms of worldliness, but retained some sin for which they had a particular weakness or a special liking. Some, in sorrow for their sins and in anxiety to get rid of them, crept through tight apertures to "scrape off" their sins.[24] In the hearts of many there was uncertainty; they lacked a cleansed conscience and the peace resulting from faith in Christ. They were Pliables, Presumptions, Talkatives, Mistrusts who turned back on their pilgrimages or did not walk on the right road to the Celestial City.

The religionists were not left unmolested. Some of the lesser clergymen considered the spiritual agitation dangerous, and advocated the suppression of the private religious gatherings. An ancient law, of 1726, was invoked, and legal proceedings were sometimes instituted against laymen. In some cases they were fined for having religious meetings in their homes. And they observed, naturally enough, that when people gathered to drink and dance and carouse, they were left unmolested, but when they themselves gathered to pray and to praise God, they were considered law-breakers and were haled before the courts.[25]

[23] M. A. Mikkelsen: "The Bishop Hill Colony," p. 20

[24] This statement is made by Emil Herlenius in his "Erik-Jansismens Historia," He refers the reader to "Uppsala Domkapitels bref till kongl. Maj:t, U. E. 11 Mars 1845," and to Ekman: "Den inre, missionens historia," p. 802.

[25] Emil Herlenius: "Erik-Jansismens Historia," p. 3.

A man playing a prominent part among the religionists from about 1825 to 1845 was Jonas Olson. He was born on the 19th of February,[26] 1802, in Soderala parish, Helsingland. His father was a drunkard, and the condition in his home seems not to have been of the best. In 1825 he undertook the management of the home farm, and at about the same time he married. After a short time—a year and a half—his wife died. This bereavement affected him deeply. His thoughts took a more serious trend. He began eagerly to study various religious books, and he joined himself to the religionists. He made yearly visits to Stockholm on business, and there he met the famous C. O. Rosenius and the noted George Scott—an English Methodist preacher and the founder of the Methodist Church in Sweden. The sermons of Scott made a deep impression upon Olson, and although he never formally joined the Methodist Church, he nevertheless came to agree with most of her tenets. Scott visited Helsingland several times, and through his efforts Olson's brother, the Olof Olson who was later sent to prospect for the intended colony, was won to the side of the religionists, among whom he together with his brother came to occupy a position of leadership. The two brothers laid stress on the importance of daily sanctification, and, partly due to Methodistic influence, they held the belief that men in this life can attain to a state of such intrinsic perfection that they are no longer guilty of any sin. They held religious gatherings not only in their home locality, but in neighboring parishes as well. Often, at their meetings, occurred fanatical episodes. But the brothers were popular and won great approval.[27]

One day in January, 1843—it was a Saturday—Jonas Olson received a visitor destined to exert over him a remarkable influence. The stranger had flour for sale, but he came also, he said, to meet brothers and sisters in Christ. Olson received him with suspicion, doubting, he said, "that anything

[26] According to Eric Johnson and C. F. Peterson: "Svenskarne i Illinois," p. 313.
[27] For an account of the religionists see Emil Herlenius: "Erik-Jansismens Historia," pp. 1-6. I am indebted to him for most of the facts in the preceding paragraphs on the religious condition in Sweden.

good could come from the corrupted Vestmanland and Uppland.'"[28] During the first evening little was said on religious subjects. The next morning Olson's married sister came to buy flour. The stranger said gravely: "Don't you know that today is the Sabbath? We will let alone trading till tomorrow." This remark made an impression upon Olson, and his suspicion began to give way. He proposed that the stranger go with the family to church, and he added that their pastor was not one of those who favored the religionists; but we attend nevertheless, said he, so as not to cause offense. The stranger accepted the invitation. After the service he was reserved and to Olson's surprise said not a word either about the pastor or about the sermon. On Sunday evening they attended a gathering of the religionists. Toward the end of the meeting, Olson gave his guest an opportunity to speak, saying that he considered him to be a man who had gone far forward on the narrow path. But against all expectation the stranger remained silent. And the meeting was dismissed.

Having arrived home, Olson asked of his guest what opinion he had of their meeting. The stranger replied: "I did not like it in the least. What kind of Christianity do you have here?" A long conversation followed. In serious words the stranger criticised what he deemed the shortcomings of the religionists; particularly he censured them for using devotional books of men and not holding themselves to the Bible alone. Through a servant on the farm, the stranger had previously acquainted himself with the conditions in the locality, and now he spoke with a knowledge that almost betokened omniscience. Jonas Olson listened meekly, and meekly he listened the next morning when the stranger gave him the following reproach: "Be a pastor in your house! I have been here a Saturday evening and a Sunday evening, and you have not held devotion with your people. You give your domestics food several times a day, but the word of God you

[28] Emil Herlenius in "Erik-Jansismens Historia," quotes this statement and tells of the visit, pp. 13-15.

do not offer them. What kind of Christian are you, who so far forget your duties as head of the house?—You have no doubt converted many from darkness to light and from the power of Satan unto God, but it has taken place according to the way we read in Hosea 7:16; they have not converted themselves rightly according to the Scriptures.''[29] Olson was deeply impressed by the stranger. He formed a high opinion of his Christianity and of his spiritual insight. Henceforth he was among the staunchest followers of the new religionist.

For the stranger did win followers. He was from now on to play an important part in the life of many a layman. He did not long remain silent in the gatherings of the religionists. And even on this first[30] visit he won, in many places, great approval. And he was to make several visits later. People were soon to flock to his meetings; the churches were soon to stand empty.[31] Inside of three years he was to become known throughout Sweden, and more than a thousand people were to consider him a prophet.[32] He was to denounce the favorite authors of the religionists as propagators of devilish doctrines. He was to lead on his followers to burn their erstwhile dearly beloved devotional books and the hymn book of the church. He was to bring strife into many homes. He was to sunder families with his preaching. He was to be persecuted, and his followers were to be persecuted with him. Several times he was to be imprisoned. He was to flee from place to place, sometimes in disguise. The stranger was Eric Janson. He was to claim himself a ''Godsent prophet,'' ''the restorer of the true doctrine,'' ''the greatest light since the time of the Apostles,''[33] the vicar of Christ on earth.[34]

---

[29] Emil Herlenius: "Erik-Jansismens Historia," p. 15.

[30] A writer calls attention to the fact that according to Eric Johnson: "Svenskarne i Illinois," p. 24, Eric Janson made a visit to Helsingland in the spring of the previous year, 1842. This may be a mistake, or if correct, the visit seems to have had no consequences.

[31] John Swainson: "Swedish Colony at Bishopshill, Illinois," in O. N. Nelson's "History of the Scandinavians and Successful Scandinavians in the United States," p. 140.

[32] Harald Wieselgren in "Biografiskt Lexicon ofer namnkunnige svenske man," given in E. Norelius: "De Svenska Lutherska Forsamlingarnes och Svenskarnes Historia i Amerika," p. 61.

[33] Emil Herlenius: "Erik-Jansismen i Sverige," p. 10.

[34] Emil Herlenius: "Erik-Jansismens Historia," p. 112.

II.

Personal History of Eric Janson Until the Beginning of His Career as Religious Leader.

The parents of Eric Janson were Johannes Mattson and Sara, née Erickson.[35] They were peasants, and during their first fifteen or eighteen years of wedded life, they were poor; but Jan was a hard-working man and improved his circumstances. Four sons and one daughter were born to them: Johan, Eric, Peter, Carl, and Anna Katarina. According to what Eric Janson himself said of his parents, they were "lovers of the world and the things that are in the world, and did not understand what God demanded of them." But according to the testimony of others, among them the youngest son Carl, they were God-fearing and diligent people who brought up their children in a strict manner. It is said that during the meals the Bible and religious questions were standing topics for conversation. It has also been said that they were not free from a taint of pride and self-conceit, traits which were claimed to be characteristic likewise of the whole kin. Jan Mattson lived till 1843. His wife died three years later on her way to the Bishop Hill Colony.

Eric Janson was the second son in the family. He was born on the 19th of December, 1808, in Bishopskulla parish in Uppland, three Swedish miles southwest from Upsala.[36] Of the four brothers he was given unquestionably the greatest natural gifts. Two incidents in his early childhood are worthy of note. The one took place when he was in his second year.[37] He was often left in the care of his brother Johan, five years older than he. One day Johan, manipulating an ax, came accidentally to mutilate two fingers on Eric's left hand.

[35] I have built this account of Eric Janson's years of minority upon Eric Johnson and C. F. Peterson: "Svenskarne i Illinois," p. 22 fl., and particularly upon Emil Herlenius: "Erik-Jansismens Historia," p. 7 fl., from which some of my account has been translated.

[36] Norelius: "De Svenska Lutherska Forsamlingarnes och Svenskarnes Historia i America," p. 61, in the article by Harald Wieselgren.

[37] Philip J. Stoneberg in Henry Kiner's "History of Henry County, Illinois," vol. 1, p. 621.

The other incident, of far greater consequence, occurred when Eric was about eight years old. At his father's command he was to do some driving with a horse and wagon. The horse became frightened, the wagon upset, and the boy was badly hurt. For several weeks he hovered between life and death. And for a number of years afterwards he was troubled with a severe headache. The accident seems to have had a great influence upon his psychic condition. He was henceforth not like other children. He avoided playmates of his own age and sought out lonely places where he at times spent hours in tears and prayers. He claimed to be unhappier than other children; for he could not do as they: romp and play. One could, indeed, weep for him.

He went to his first communion when seventeen years of age, and now for a time there came to him somewhat happier days. At this time he read his Bible and other religious books, but without any great zest, however, and soon he discontinued his reading. The old uneasiness and anxiety took hold upon him again. To find relief, he took part at times in dancing and in other amusements of the young. His parents disapproved of his "scruples," and set him to hard work. As a result, his health suffered and he became subject to very painful rheumatism.

And so time went on till the summer of 1830 when he was in his twenty-second year. At this time is said to have taken place his real conversion. He tells the story himself. One day, though greatly troubled with his rheumatism, he rode out with a span of horses to work on the farm. The pains became unbearable, and, falling off the horse, he remained for a while on the ground, powerless. Then he heard a voice saying: "It is written that whatsoever you ask in prayer, believing, that shall be given unto you, and all things are possible for him who believes, and when you call, I will answer you, says the Lord." He got up on his knees and prayed long and earnestly, and from this hour he was forever free from his malady.[38]

[38] Transcribed from Emil Herlenius: "Erik-Jansismens Historia," p. 8.

On the very next day he began to preach the word of God to those about him. He began also with great eagerness to read all the religious literature that he could lay his hands on. At this time he meditated much on the eternal suffering of the condemned. There were some people in the locality who maintained that there would be no such punishment, but Janson rejected their belief positively. At this time, also, he wrote some religious verses and essays under the title, "Words of Warning to a World in Sin, etc."[39] These writings reveal a humble attitude of mind, a clear realization of man's weakness on account of sin, and a heartfelt thankfulness for the grace of God. In addition to the Bible, some of his favorite books were at this time the writings of Luther, Arndt, Nohrborg, and Murbeck.[40]

In this way, four years went by. Then a change took place in the life of Eric Janson. He discontinued completely to preach the word of God. He himself tells of the reason for this change. "I read much," he says, "in Johan Arndt's 'True Christianity'; for he had a reputation for truth and Christianity. This devilish book deceived me woefully so that unwittingly I fell into this sin of no longer preaching. Indeed, Arndt told me that I should remain quietly in my calling and not aspire to become a teacher, nor should I, who had tilled the soil, seek to preach. This devilish doctrine I accepted after I was satiated with the revilings which daily came upon me on account of my preaching among the people. I began to think that there might be teachers in the world whom I did not know, and thus it was superfluous for me to preach the Gospel of Christ to the people.[41] He adds that also Luther taught him that they who are peasants must always consider whether or not they are by the spirit of God called to preach. The period during which Janson refrained from preaching lasted for about six years.

---

[39] Title in Swedish: "Varingsord till en Syndareverld, m. m."

[40] Emil Herlenius: "Erik-Jansismens Historia," p. 9.

[41] From Janson's Autobiography, as quoted by Emil Herlenius in his "Erik-Jansismens Historia," p. 11.

When Janson was in his twenty-seventh year—about the time he quit preaching—he married a girl who shared his liking for Bible-reading, one Maria Kristina Larson, a servant girl in his parent's house. For a long time the parents had opposed the union, and the consequence was that the circumstances impelled them to marry. The young couple moved now to Voppeby and settled down on a leased farm. As he had been industrious at home in his father's house and had done much of his Bible reading at night so as not to take away any time from his labor on the farm, so he was industrious now in this rented place, and soon he gained the reputation of being the most efficient farmer in the neighborhood. In addition to farming, he tried his luck as a dealer in flour. And although there were serious crop failures, he managed so well that after about four years on the place, he could buy a home of his own. This he did near Sankarby in Osterunda parish. He bought the new place for one thousand riks-dollars, and he was able to pay for it in cash. In this new home he remained in quietness for about two years. True, he showed at times a liking for controversy and an inclination to believe himself better able than other people to understand the Scriptures. But according to reliable testimony he tended his farm faithfully, read the Bible diligently, visited—more frequently than most people—the Lord's table, lived an irreproachable life, evinced a more serious Christianity than the majority of those about him. And although he felt burning in his heart a desire to speak the word of God, yet, during these six years, he did not preach.

Then in 1840 there occurred something which Janson himself designated as his second conversion. In the fall of that year he went with his youngest brother to Upsala to sell cattle. The ungodly life of the people at the market made a deep impression upon him, and he felt the call to preach repentance. Upon his return he consulted his pastor, relating what had taken place during the ten years that he had walked the narrow way. He felt power and ability to preach, he said, but Arndt and Luther told him to remain silent. The pastor urged him strongly to preach. And Eric Janson began once more to proclaim the word of God.[42]

The religionists were having meetings in Janson's neighborhood, and he began now to appear at these gatherings as a speaker. The two pastors in the congregation both encouraged him, and for about two years he continued to preach in his home locality. He was favorably received, and his pastors recommended him highly. But little by little there began to be apparent in his preaching a drifting away from the Lutheran doctrine. He had come to believe, in the first place, that the true Christian has no longer any sin. The believer is free from sin, not only in the sense that he is made clean through the blood of Christ, or in the sense that he is righteous in the sight of God by virtue of the attributed righteousness of Christ, but he is free from sin also in this sense that he is no longer guilty of any slips and shortcomings. At any rate, the Christian would not be guilty of the same sin twice.—In the next place, he had come to hold that the Bible was the only religious book for Christians to read. He had developed a strong hatred for the writings of Luther and Arndt—to mention no others. Religious literature, outside of the Bible, was a work of man, and should not be studied.—A third tenet, which he came to announce by and by more boldly as time went on, was this: He was sent of God to be a preacher of the true doctrine. His "usual public declarations on this point were these: 'The new doctrine I teach is of God; I am sent by God.'"[43] There was one God, and Eric Janson was his prophet.—At the end of two years of preaching in his home locality, Janson seems to have been losing in popularity. He was getting ripe, now, for beginning his career as leader of a separate religious sect. He was soon ready to begin that work concerning which a man who knew him personally and who was never antagonistic toward him uttered the following words: "No matter in how favorable a light I might wish to view the matter, the Eric-Jansonist movement in our province

[42] See Emil Herlenius: "Erik-Jansismens Historia," p. 11 fl.
[43] E. W. Olson: "History of the Swedes of Illinois," vol. 1, p. 203, footnote.

can never be regarded as one of these grace-giving winds from the Lord which blow life into the dead bones, but must be regarded as one of these violent storms, typhoons, which at times pass over the equatorial regions and which, indeed, disrupt sundry decaying things and in that way are of use, yet which at the same time tear up much that ought to be preserved and in that way effect a great deal of damage."[44]

III.

Eric Janson's Career as Religious Leader in Sweden.

Before we follow up the career of Eric Janson as a religious leader, it would be well if we could form a mental picture of the man. He is described[45] as having been of middle height, or taller. His complexion was pallid, his face thin, his chin rounded, his nose straight and pointed. His cheekbones were prominent, his cheeks sunken, his lips thin and closely drawn. His teeth, especially the upper front teeth, were unusually long and wide. He had a deep scar across the forehead. His hair was brown. He had blue eyes, and it is said that in those eyes he had an almost hypnotic power. He wore a leer continually, but it has been suggested that this was possibly due to an involuntary contraction of the muscles. The first two fingers on his left hand were cut off. When he had something to say of special importance, he would embrace the person to whom he said it, man or woman irrespectively. If he discovered a fault in a person, he was ready at the first opportunity to call his attention to it. "His personality was such as to admit of no mediocre opposition." "He was a man of large social affections and, where religion did not interfere with the dictates of nature, of quick and ready sympathies."

[44] As additional source for the above paragraph see Emil Herlenius: "Erik-Jansismens Historia," pp. 11-13; p. 21, and p. 115.

[45] I have gathered the following description from Emil Herlenius: "Erik-Jansismens Historia," p. 27; M. A. Mikkelsen: "The Bishop Hill Colony," p. 45; and Philip J. Stoneberg's article on the Bishop Hill Colony, found in Henry L. Kiner's: "History of Henry County, Illinois," vol. 1, pp. 621-651.

We have heard already something of Janson's first visit to Helsingland. With this visit began a new epoch in the career of this singular man. When he left Olson's, he proceeded northward, preached in a number of places, and met with some opposition and with much approval. In Norrala he became acquainted with Norin, the leader among the laymen at that place. Norin at first favored him, but after a time became convinced that the stranger was a false teacher. As the two men parted, Norin requested Janson never to visit the place again. Highly provoked, Janson said: "May Norrala be as a scorched mountain on which nothing grows!" "The judgment is hard," replied Norin, "but I think that pronounced by the lips of Eric Janson it is of no consequence."[46]—But opposition to Janson was not the general thing. At this time he departed but slightly in his preaching from the common tenets of the religionists, and "he shrewdly concealed his antipathy to the writings of Luther, Arndt, Nohrborg and others."[47] And for the most part he met with success. He received approval even from clergymen. He came home in the middle of February and was cordially received by his pastor, "who, however, warned him against spiritual arrogance."[48]

Eric Janson was highly gifted as an orator. He could express himself with the utmost readiness. He had strong self-confidence and a giant memory. He was well at home in the Bible, and could quote from it very readily. He had strong dialectic abilities, and he was able to speak four or five hours in a stretch without exhaustion. His voice, however, was not pleasant. It was extremely harsh, rather weak than strong, and sounded as though he were talking with something in his mouth. When giving his public discourses, he was in the habit of keeping his eyes closed, or so nearly closed that only the whites were visible. He seemed to have the ability to shed tears at will. "He did not hesitate to punish in public the sins of prominent individuals." His preaching was legal-

[46] For this incident and for the story of Janson's preaching on the first visit to Helsingland, see Emil Herlenius: "Erik-Jansismens Historia," p. 15-17.

[47] E. W. Olson: "History of the Swedes of Illinois," vol. 1, p. 204.

[48] Ibid, p. 204.

istic. Many who had believed themselves Children of God before, came to believe, when they heard Janson, that, after all, they had deceived themselves. "His style of preaching and method of delivery is said to have resembled very much that of the early Methodists." He exerted an almost irresistible control over his audience. There were people who declared that they were strongly hostile to him and that they had gone to his meetings for no other purpose than to cause disturbance. But when he looked them in the eye and in earnestness spoke a few words to them, he gained mastery over them almost against their will. His followers at last went so far in their devotion to him that they declared themselves willing to follow him into death, yea, to hell itself, if he were to go there.[49]

After his second visit to Helsingland, while he was at his home in Osterunda parish, Janson had, he declared, a vision similar to the one of King Solomon. He asked, as did Solomon, that he might be given "an understanding heart to judge thy people, that I may discern between good and evil." And, according to his own assertion, he received what is mentioned in 1 Kings, 3, 12. This verse reads: "Behold, I have done according to thy word: lo, I have given thee a wise and an understanding heart; so that there hath been none like thee before thee, neither after thee shall any arise like unto thee." "The story of my life,' said Janson, "as well as everything which proceeds according to the Scriptures, shall testify to this until the Day of Judgment and afterward in eternity."[50]

After a great deal of success as a preacher, Janson attempted to be also a miraculous healer. On his third visit to Helsingland he tried to restore to health an elderly maid who had been confined to her bed for years. He urged her to take him by the hand and to say "I believe," and she would then be healed of her sickness. She finally consented. He then turned to those about him and began to praise God for what had taken place, saying that he had driven out the evil

[49] The above description of Janson's characteristics as a preacher I have built mainly on Emil Herlenius: "Erik-Jansismens Historia," pp. 15, 16, 26, 27; and on M. A. Mikkelsen: "The Bishop Hill Colony," pp. 16 and 20.

[50] Emil Herlenius: "Erik-Jansismens Historia," p. 20.

spirit. The sick said, "He is mistaken," and turned to the wall. Shortly afterward, Janson sent a letter to Osterunda in which he spoke of having driven out demons from two women.[51]—Another attempt at miraculous healing is told of as follows: "In Kalkbo, Forsa parish, there was a young man aged twenty-nine, a cripple who had been bedridden from childhood. After having made the house his headquarters for some time, Eric Janson attempted to heal him in a miraculous manner. He predicted that on midsummer day (1844) the young man, suddenly cured of the malady, would 'leap like a young deer.' The invalid and his family firmly believed this, and clothes were ordered for him, but when the day arrived, there was no perceptible change in his condition. The failure cost Eric Janson a number of adherents, and the house was closed to him from that day."[52]

After his third visit to Helsingland, Janson began to make preparations to move thither for good. He was prompted to do so on account of his success in that place and no doubt also on account of the animosity which met him at home—not least from his parents and brothers. He sold his home in Osterunda for nine hundred rik-s—dollars. At about this time, in November, 1843, his father died. Janson then, instead of moving to Helsingland at once, took up his temporary abode on the parental farm. He made a fourth visit to Helsingland, bringing with him also this time wheat flour for sale. Having returned home, and having sold his share in the parental farm, he was ready to move to Helsingland in April, 1844. With his wife and two children, Eric and Mathilda—two children had previously died in their infancy—he settled down finally at Stenbo in Forssa, in the northern part of Helsingland.[53]

At about this time his followers began to form a separate party—the Eric-Jansonists. Many of them had been religion ists also before Janson's activity. They now claimed posi

[51] From Emil Herlenius: "Erik-Jansismens Historia," p. 21.
[52] From Landgren, as related by E. W. Olson in "History of the Swedes of Illinois," vol. 1, p. 207.
[53] For the facts in this paragraph and for an account of Janson's activity on his fourth visit see Emil Herlenius: "Erik-Jansismens Historia," pp. 21-23.

tively that their leader "was sent of God to show them the right way to heaven," and that "neither the dean nor his adjunct preached the Word rightly." Janson himself asserted at one time that none could have been saved through the preaching which had been proclaimed previously. One Sunday he attended the regular services in the church and went to communion. In the evening of the same day he said that in the forenoon "he had heard a devilish sermon and had received the Lord's Supper from the devil himself. Luther and those who spoke like him preached so miserably that "if a devil had come up from hell, he could not have preached worse." He forbade his followers to attend services in the churches; they were instead to come to his own meetings, which were regularly held at the same hour.[54]

Janson was not sparing in his denounciations of his opponents. He found fault with many of the religionists and also with pastors in sympathy with them. At first the latter were dubbed "not true Christians," "idols," "hirelings." By and by they were given to understand that they were "whitewashers, pillars in hell and the arch-purveyors of the devil." "The whole clergy," he said, "with bishops and everything, is the clergy of the devil." If anyone was bold enough to oppose him in his meetings, he would be apt, if he did not soon hold his peace, to be silenced with some such expression as the following: "You are of the devil." "Such a devil we have in the midst of our gathering." "You are so full of devils that if they crept out of you, the house would be full." At one meeting he was interrupted by a twelve year old girl, a niece of Jonas Olson. How are we then to understand, she asked, what we read concerning Job? When his suffering was severe, he cursed his birthday. Was not that sin? Yet, God calls him "My servant Job." Since God calls him his servant, was he not faithful? For once in his life, Janson did not seem to have an answer ready-made. He became confused, paged about in the Bible, and said, "Let see, let see." Finally he said: "I shall answer you on that some other time." But

[54] Emil Herlenius: "Erik-Jansismens Historia," pp. 23, 24, 28, 34 and 35.

when several persons urged him to answer the question at once, he became angry and said: "Take the devil out!" To a person who had been without avail both coaxed and threatened in order that he might join the Jansonists, the prophet finally exclaimed: "All authority hath been given unto me in heaven and on earth. If I so willed, you should at once fall dead at my feet and go to hell!"[55]

Nor was Janson backward in claiming for himself an important place in the stewardship of God. "I preach," he said, "not as the scribes, but with might and power. You, if you believe my words, shall know that my words are spirit and life, and that you need not seek life far away from you, but nearby in power." He claimed to be inspired by the Holy Spirit, and to be sent of God to restore the true doctrine. "As sure as God is God," he said, "it is the Spirit of God the Father who speaks through me." He styled himself a "God-sent prophet," and he said: "Since the time of the Apostles, there has been found no true preacher before me."[56] "God has determined," he asserted, "to reveal through me his mysteries." At last he considered himself as standing in the place of Christ on earth, and he applied to himself Bible passages like these: "I am the good shepherd, "I am the true vine," "All authority hath been given unto me in heaven and on earth." His writings abound with expressions to the effect that he is sent of God and that he has a likeness to Christ. "Eric Janson has said in Christ's stead, as God said in the hour of creation: Be light—and there was light." "This is the work of God to believe on me who stands in Christ's stead and has been given in hands all the riches that Jesus Christ has received by the glorious power of his Father." "Therefore, he who does not abide in me shall be cast forth as a branch and shall wither." The glory which Eric Janson establishes in Christ's stead shall surpass the glory wrought by Jesus and his apostles in all lands. The coming of Christ

[55] Emil Herlenius: "Erik-Jansismens Historia." pp. 25, 26, 33, 48, 24, note 5. The last incident was related to Mr. Herlenius by the very girl in question. She was then an old woman.

[56] C. A. Cornelius: "Svenska Kyrkans Historia Efter Reformationen," vol. 2, p. 207.

is revealed in its height through Eric Janson's obedience before God, On that account salvation is to be found only through him. "To doubt the one whom God has sent is the greatest idolatry that the Word of God mentions; for the one who touches him touches the apple of the eye of God. No greater sin can be committed under the sun." The one whom God sent is to be honored as Jesus himself, and in case Janson suffers death at the hands of murderers as Jesus did, the faithful must also take care of his family as the Apostle John did of the mother of Christ.[57]

To prove, said Eric Janson, that he was sent by God was in reality not necessary. Christ, too, had declared when he was asked by some of the scribes to give them a sign: "There shall no sign be given,"—Janson left out the words "but the sign of Jonah the prophet." Nevertheless, both Janson himself and his followers spoke of proofs to the effect that he was sent by God. When he was arrested the first time, he said as he parted from his friends: "If I come back to you without anyone having been able to do me any harm, you shall thereby know that I am sent of God."—At one time he said: "I have written a hymn of fifteen verses in one and a half hour without having anything to copy from; I can go into God in secret and say: 'Give me what I need.' But the learned, teachers and bishops, must sit and scratch their head for every line. But I am not the one who does this; it is the Spirit of God the Father, who dwells in me. To him belongs the honor for it."—At one time when some doubt had been expressed as to whether Janson was in his right mind, he considered this a strong proof of his spiritual call; for Christ had said that those who confessed him should be considered mad.[58]—At another time, when he returned from one of his arrests, a Jansonist said in glee: "What further need have we of witnesses?"[59]—To prove further that he was a man of God, both

[57] If not otherwise designated most of the statements in this paragraph have been taken from Emil Herlenius: "Erik-Jansismens Historia," pp. 17, note, 22, 24, 33, 112, 113. Herlenius has quoted many of the statements from Janson's Catechism. Some of the statements not in quotation marks have been translated or transcribed from Herlenius.

[58] Gefleborgs Lans Tidning," 1844, No. 97; quoted by Emil Herlenius: "Erik-Jansismens Historia," p. 36.

[59] Emil Herlenius: "Erik-Jansismens Historia," pp. 30, 33, 47.

Janson and his adherents used to reason as follows: "The Scriptures nowhere speak of only one false prophet or one false apostle, but always of more than one. Thus, Eric Jansen, being only one, since nobody alone against all teachers as Micaiah stood alone against the four hundred false prophets."[60]

Eric Janson, in spite of his doctrine of perfect sinlessness, was not above reproach. He was several times accused of improper relations with some of his women followers. One of the women in question was Sophie Schon. "One night she was surprised . . . by the pastor of Osterunda Parish, who had come with a number of his henchmen to find Eric Janson. Eric Janson was, of course, not to be found; but Sophia Schon was dragged from her bed and brought, dressed only in her linen, to the sheriff's bailiff."[61]—At one time in Soderala Eric Janson received publicly a strong admonition from Karin Olson—a sister of Jonas and Olof Olson—because he was said to stand in improper relationship to a married woman in the same parish.[62]—Another story is told as follows: "One woman, who with her husband was then devoted to the prophet, afterwards said of Eric Janson and the Bolnas girl: 'Their wanton and unchaste behavior made me blush on behalf of our sex.' "[63]—Janson's own wife several times accused him of unfaithfulness. To persons who heard the upbraidings, he was wont to say: "All this I get on account of your unbelief; for because you do not have faith, Satan has received power to sift her as wheat."[64]—At one time, on a Sunday evening, he made an unchaste solicitation to Karin Erson. He added that he never until now wished to lose his wife, but now it wouldn't matter; for had he known Karin beforehand, he would have had her for wife. Eric Janson was forced to acknowledge in the presence of several witnesses that Karin's statement of the case was correct. At one time when urged by Olof Olson

[60] The quotations in this paragraph are taken from Emil Herlenius: "Erik-Jansismens Historia," pp. 30, 33, and 113.
[61] M. A. Mikkelsen: "The Bishop Hill Colony," p. 22. Herlenius speaks of the same incident in "Erik-Jansismens Historia," p. 50 fl.
[62] Emil Herlenius: "Erik-Jansismens Historia," p. 27.
[63] E. W. Olson: "History of the Swedes of Illinois," vol. 1, p. 209.
[64] P. N. Lundquist: "Erik-Jansismen i Helsingland," Gefle 1845. Referred to in Emil Herlenius: "Erik-Jansismen i Sverige," p. 25, note 2.

to justify himself in this matter, he said: "It was a punishment from God upon me because I had for some days believed that Magister Sefstrom was a true Christian, and this was a great sin."[65] Having admitted that Karin's statement was correct, he later declared that he had spoken thus only to test her virtue. He publicly pronounced the severest curses upon her, and maintained that already previous to this affair she was known for her immoral life. He asserted that she and a certain pastor, whom he mentioned by name, had sustained an improper relationship to each other and that she had attempted to establish a similar relationship to him. He also tried by severe threatenings to make Karin retract her assertion, but to no avail.[66] Those stories were not, however, able to shake, in any degree worth mentioning, the faith of the Jansonists in their leader. On the contrary, they defended him saying: "Even though Eric Janson did this and that, his heart was nevertheless righteous before God, no matter what the body does."[67]

As time went on Eric Janson became more and more outspoken in his denunciations of religious books. "All books," he said, "are idols which ought to be burnt." He raged most of all against the writings of Luther and Arndt. "The idols from which the heart is to be cleansed," he declared, "are first and foremost the idolatrous books, particularly Luther's and Arndt's." The teachings of these men were "not the Gospel of God, but a devilish gospel, a devilish water which he let flow over the whole world." The Jansonists came to the conclusion that they needed "only one God and one book." To burn man-made religious books would be to promote the spiritual welfare both of themselves and of their fellowmen. And so at last the Jasonists were ready for a public burning of books. For several days a great number of people from various places brought together books and heaped them up at the seashore for a big bonfire. As yet the hymn

[65] Emil Herlenius: "Erik-Jansismens Historia," p. 105, note. He refers also to P. N. Lundquist: "Erik-Jansismen i Helsingland," p. 165, note.

[66] Emil Herlenius: "Erik-Jansismen i Sverige," p. 11 and "Erik-Jansismens Historia," p. 26fl. and p. 105, note. E. W. Olson also tells the story in his "History of the Swedes of Illinois," and bases it upon Lundgren: "Erik-Jansismen," p. 29.

[67] Upsala Domkapitels arkiv: "Handlingar rorande forsamlingarna inom erkestiftet," quoted by Emil Herlenius: "Erik-Jansismen i Sverige," p. 12.

book and Luther's Catechism were spared, although they were designated respectively as "Satan's ditties" and "an empty barrel with two bottoms." But the postils of Luther, Arndt, Nohrborg, Linderoth, and of many others were in the heap. And so, of course, was Arndt's "True Christianity." A great number of books on temperance were also consigned to the flames. The value of the books was about 975 riks-dollars. The burning took place on the 11th of June, 1844. Eric Janson himself was present and encouraged his followers with words like these: "Satan had a jubilee when Luther's writings were published; now, when they are burnt, he will have to be in mourning." Those who were along at the burning were promised "a heavenly joy when the smoke of the idols arose." Some desired to take the covers off form the books that once had been so dear to them, but the prophet declared, "Cursed be each and every one who takes the covers off the idols!" When the crowd saw the books curl and open in the flames, they called out, "See how Satan gapes!" To the assembled throng Eric Janson read the eighteenth chapter of the Apocalypse. It treats of the fall and desolation of Babylon: "In one day shall her plagues come, death, and mourning, and famine; and she shall be utterly burned with fire; for strong is the Lord God who judged her." Two peasant boys shouted: "Thank and praise the Lord!" And the crowd responded: "To the Lord be thanks and praise!" The books were burned. But the promised heavenly joy did not come to those who took part. On the contrary, a feeling of depression, somehow, took possession of the crowd.—A second burning of books took place in October of the same year. Now the hymn book—at least the one that had been in use formerly—was not spared, nor was Luther's Catechism. They were in the near future to be supplanted by something better; for Janson had promised that he would soon publish a catechism and a hymn book both written by himself.—There were also other and minor burnings at which the prophet was not present.[68]

[68] This paragraph has been built upon Emil Herlenius: "Erik-Jansismen i Sverige," pp. 15 fl., 20, 22; and "Erik-Jansismens Historia," pp. 28-30, 34, 39, 40, 41.

On the day after the first burning of books, an attempt was made to arrest Eric Janson, but the attempt failed. On the following day the efforts were renewed. The sheriff, assisted by a military man and by fifty or sixty other robust fellows, came to apprehend the prophet. The followers of Janson defended him fiercely. When at last he was cornered, the feeling against him was so bitter that some even proposed to end his life. The affair did not go to this extreme, however; he was instead outraged and mistreated and sent off to jail. While in the hands of the authorities, he was examined both as to his sanity and as to his orthodoxy. He was sent from one place to another, and even had audience with the king. From Stockholm he wrote to his followers in Helsingland and ordered some of them to come to him and others to go out and preach his doctrine. In his command he called attention to these words in the Bible: "There is no man that hath left house, or brethren, or sisters, or mother, or father, or children, or lands, for my sake, and for the gospel's sake, but he shall receive a hundredfold now in this time, houses, and brethren, and sisters, and mothers, and children, and lands, with persecutions; and in the world to come eternal life." From Stockholm he went to Vesteras where he received a pass and permission to return to Helsingland. The prophet was again free.[69]

And now he appeared with still greater boldness than before. From this time on he began to compare himself to the Savior. Surrounded by eleven men and a great number of women, he went from village to village. At his gatherings there was read "The Passion Story of Eric Janson." It told of his deeds and sufferings since the time of his arrest. It told how he had been sentenced to roast over a slow fire and afterward to be beheaded. It told how, repeatedly, he had been dragged before the courts, but how none had been able to do him any harm. For he had been delivered from all molestation, both now and for the future, through a particularly intimate acquaintanceship with the king, before whom he had

[69] Emil Herlenius: "Erik-Jansismens Historia," pp. 30-32.

freely proclaimed that the Lutheran doctrine was a false doctrine. This avowal had saved him, and His Majesty had not only promised him protection, but had even so far agreed with him as to say that "he did not regard the Lutheran clergy higher than the louse on a calf." Now Janson was provided with the king's seal that he might go about and teach the people.—And the reputation of the prophet was higher than ever before.[70]

Eric Janson was several times arrested and several times set free. He did not cease preaching, and people came in ever-increasing numbers to hear "the voice of one crying in the wilderness." In these tumultuous times he began to ordain and to send out preachers or apostles to proclaim his doctrine. An eye-witness tells of one of these ordinations in substance as follows: After the young man who was to be ordained had given a discourse, Eric Janson stepped forth and said that the person in question had "received the spirit and that, too, not by measure." Therefore the office of instructorship in the congregation ought not to be withheld from him. Thereupon Janson placed his hands upon the candidate and prayed: "O thou God of our fathers, I thank thee that thou hast always heard me; and so I know also that thou always hearest me; but because of the multitude that standeth around I say it, that they may believe that thou didst send me. Oh, pour down the grace of Thy spirit upon this my colleague as upon Thy apostles on the first day of Pentecost! —Peace be with you! Receive the Holy Spirit; whose soever sins you forgive, they are forgiven unto them; whose soever sins you retain, they are retained. Yea, I give unto you the keys of the kingdom of heaven; whatsoever you shall bind on earth shall be bound in heaven, and whatsoever you loose on earth shall be loosed in heaven." The benediction was pronounced; the people sang a hymn; and the ceremony was over.[71]

---

[70] Transcribed from Emil Herlenius: "Erik-Jansismens Historia," pp. 32 fl.

[71] P. E. Frisk in letter to Landgren, referred to by Emil Herlenius: "Erik-Jansismens Historia," p. 48. The original letter is in the "prostarkiv" in Delsbo.

Eric Janson was a prophet not only in the sense that he proclaimed the word of God, as he thought, but also in the sense that he attempted to foretell events. A prophesy current among the Jansonists asserted that inside of two years, the whole world should be converted to their belief, and those who had withstood them should then be destroyed.—In the summer of 1845 the rumor spread that in answer to the prophet's prayer it would not rain for three years and six months. When rain nevertheless fell in July, it was said that the prophet out of compassion had through a new prayer removed the effect of the first.—If Janson "failed in his attempts as prophet and wonderworker, he was always ready to throw the blame upon the unbelief of others and by that means save his repute."[72]

As Janson clashed with the church, so of course did his followers.—One of the chief tenets of Jansonism was that the Christian is no longer guilty of any sin. Hence it would be but empty words and mockery for a Jansonist to read the common confession of sins at the communion table. The only way in which he could conscientiously do this would be to think of the sins committed before he became a Christian. The pastors, on their side, according to the law of the church, could not let the Jansonists receive the Lord's Supper without this confession. And so the Jansonists often communed in their own way in their own gatherings.—For another thing, the Jansonists insisted upon having their own meetings at the time of the regular Sunday services. "For," said some of them, "since the word of God commands that we should in season and out of season read the word of God, reprove, rebuke, and exhort, there is no time to discontinue therewith during the public church-service."[73] As a result of this refusal to attend services in the Established Church, some of the Jansonists were summoned before the authorities and had to pay fines for neglected church-going. Furthermore, in one parish a law was passed to the effect that anyone who opened

[72] Emil Herlenius: "Erik-Jansismens Historia," p. 51, note, and p. 112.
[73] Upsala Domkapitels arkiv: "Protokollsboker," June 18, 1845. Quoted by Emil Herlenius: "Erik-Jansismens Historia," p. 45.

his house to the meetings of the Jansonists should be subject to a fine. At one time Jonas Olson and his brother Olof each had to pay a fine of more than sixty-six riks-dollars for having held unlawful meetings.—One Jansonist is spoken of who refused before the authorities to desist in his attempts to urge members to fall away from their congregation.—It also happened that Jansonists refused to send their children to school; for they would not let the fallacies of Luther's Catechism be inculcated to their children. Eric Janson had promised to have ready a catechism of his own, and the children could wait going to school till they could be taught the true doctrine.—In some places the Jansonists were highly hostile also to the civil authority. It happened several times that they were not accepted as witnesses in court for the reason that they had wrong ideas concerning the doctrine of salvation and could not have a right conception as to the importance of the oath. It is not difficult to understand that such discrimination seemed to the Jansonists the most high-handed injustice.[74]

The prophet himself was, as we might expect, not the only one to be subjected to violence. Some Jansonists complained at one time in a written statement that a certain dean in the church had overwhelmed them with such harsh words and accusations that "even their adversaries thought it went too far." One pastor is known to have been so far deficient in tact and wisdom, that both in words and deeds he urged on the young people in the congregation to disturb the meetings of the Jansonists by throwing stones and by perpetrating other mischief against them. There were places, where, as time went on, the people conceived such a hatred for the Jansonists that wantonness against them knew scarcely any bounds.[75] At one time, just as the Jansonists had begun their meetings, a crowd pressed into the room and thoroughly maltreated those present, both men and women. On the following Sunday, in a different place, they were also disturbed,

[74] Emil Herlenius: "Erik-Jansismens Historia," pp. 41, 42, 50, 46, 38, 47, 51, 52, and 52, note 4.

[75] Emil Herlenius: "Erik-Jansismens Historia," pp. 43, 46, 49.

but through the speedy intervention of a magistrate they were this time saved from bodily violence. On one Sunday some Jansonists, not daring to have an hour of devotion in their own home, gathered instead at the shore of a lake. When they returned, they found that some persecutors, under pretext of searching for Eric Janson, had forced themselves into the house and had disarranged furniture and turned topsy-turvy other moveables in the house. At one service where Janson himself was present the sheriff broke in upon the meeting. The Jansonists resisted violently, urged on by the prophet. Many were hurt more or less, and clothes were torn to pieces. At last Janson was captured. His wife was also in the gathering, and during the turmoil she was so badly buffeted that she lay there for a while unconscious. At one time as Eric Janson had just begun his sermon and was encouraging his followers saying that the archbishop and other persons high in authority had come to consider his doctrine right and true and that therefore no fear need be entertained from that source, the sheriff again stepped in, followed by some eighteen lusty men. A violent tumult was soon agog. At this time Janson escaped, but his wife again fared badly. To avoid mistreatment she fled to the barn. When she saw herself pursued, she tried to escape through an aperture in the floor, but her clothes caught, and she could not get away. Some lads who saw her predicament came with switches and and gave her a sound whipping.[76] The Jansonists had ample opportunity to learn that to be different from other people is to be persecuted.

The Jansonists bore up under these persecutions both badly and bravely. As in altercations between individuals "one word leads to another," so in dissensions between parties one harsh measure from one side provokes retaliation from the other. It is human to act so, and the Jansonists, too, were human. They claimed that the clergy was the first and greatest cause for the unlawful arrests and the violent acts at which even their lives had been endangered. And so

[76] Emil Herlenius: "Erik-Jansismens Historia," pp. 47, 49, 36 fl., 49.

when, as it happened in some places, the pastors attempted to bring the Jansonists back to the congregation, the result was often nothing but spiteful and derisive words. One man declared that the pastors might as well be thrown on the muck-pile; for when the salt had lost its savor, it was good for nothing else. Another Jansonist asserted that he would gladly give his whole forest if out of the trees were made blocks and gallows for the clergy. In one parish a great number of Jansonists went from village to village holding meetings at which they heaped all kinds of revilings upon the church and the clergy, saying that all churches ought to be burnt and that all pastors ought to be hanged or have the tongue cut out of their throats. One Jansonist is said to have spit into a pastor's face, and when someone censured him for doing so, he replied, "What else should I do since the devil stands in front of me?" According to report, the Jansonists in one place asked God in their prayers that the days of the king might not be many, but that they might be given another king who would show more justice to their cause.—But although the Jansonists often gave vent to harsh thoughts and to the hate that was in their hearts, they also sought to endure the tribulations in a Christian spirit. They attempted, though not in a wise way perhaps, to do good to those who hated them and to pray for those who dispitefully used them. "They marched along the public highways at night and sang spiritual hymns, or gathered in front of their parsonages to pray for the conversion of their unregenerate pastors."[77] Both Janson himself and some of his followers expressed joy in their tribulations; for they considered that they suffered for Christ's sake. And they encouraged each other: "Be faithful unto the end."[78]

The prophet himself was at last publicly sought after. He fled from place to place and tried as much as possible to keep in hiding. Sometimes he went about disguised in a woman's dress.[79] It is even claimed that he let his two big

[77] M. A. Mikkelsen: "The Bishop Hill Colony," p. 21.

[78] From Emil Herlenius: "Erik-Jansismens Historia," pp. 45, 40 fl., 46, 55 fl., 48, 36, 42, 51.

[79] E. W. Olson: "History of the Swedes of Illinois," vol. 1, p. 216.

front teeth be broken out so as to become less easily recognizable. At one time the rumor spread that he was murdered, and it was undoubtedly to make the authorities believe this rumor that his wife appeared in a widow's dress in Gefle and asked for information concerning her dead husband. Where the murder was supposed to have taken place, a woman sprinkled the blood of a kid on the way. But it was soon understood that the whole thing was a ruse in order so much the easier to keep the prophet in hiding. At one time he was hidden in a stable.[80] At another time he lived under a barn floor for five weeks, and later for some weeks in a garret in the same parish. Nobody knew of his hiding place except those who brought him food—his wife and a former servant girl.[81]

At last the hardships were getting almost unbearable for Eric Janson and his followers. They began to think of leaving their country for a land where they should have freedom both to teach concerning God as they deemed right and to seek unhindered to win others for their doctrine. And that land of freedom was the United States. One Gustaf Flack, who was probably the first Swede in Chicago, had sent home letters in which he spoke most favorably of the new country, particularly of the religious freedom. The "America-fever" had at this time begun to spread in Sweden, and the Jansonists fell victims. In those early days America was a land practically unknown to most of the people in Sweden. "It was feared that they would be taken by pirates, or that the captains of their vessels would sell them into slavery, or bring them to the terrible 'island' of Siberia where the Czar of Russia sends all his desperate criminals. In American waters, too, there were frightful sea-monsters, more ferocious and destructive than even the Midgard serpent. And if America was the home of freedom and a country of fabulous wealth, it was also the resort of cut-throats and assassins

[80] For the facts mentioned above see Emil Herlenius: "Erik-Jansismens Historia," p. 54.

[81] Ibid, p. 50.

and full of tropical abnormities.''[82] But the Jansonists were not a faint people. They decided to emigrate.[83]

And so they began to prepare for leaving their fatherland. Olof Olson was sent to prospect in the new country for a suitable location for the emigrants. Eric Janson formed a plan according to which the emigration should take place, and soon, in advance of his adherents, he followed Olson across the sea. Some of the Jansonists were fairly well to do; others did not have enough to pay for the voyage; still others were in debt. And so, as in the first days of the Christian Church, a common fund was established. They sold their little farms and what property they had and contributed the money to this common fund. They even sold the clothes which they did not need for daily use; for all were to be dressed alike. One contributed to the common fund as much as twenty-four thousand riks-dollars. Others gave twelve thousand, five thousand, one thousand, and so on. Four men were selected to be stewards of the treasury. From this common fund ships were hired and tickets were bought for rich and poor alike. Debts were paid with money from the same fund. Some were soldiers, and from this fund they were bought free. For several of these there was paid as much as one thousand riks-dollars each. And so at last were torn off all the external bonds that held the Jansonists to their native land.[84]

When the Jansonists left Sweden, they had no hopes of ever seeing their neighbors and the country of their birth again. They had tried to win their fellowmen for the true doctrine, for Jansonism, but they would not believe the truth. And now as the Apostle Paul had turned from his own people, so would the Jansonists turn from their countrymen and go to the heathens. They compared themselves also to the Israelites leaving Egypt. They believed that as the army of Pharoah had been destroyed in the Red Sea by Moses, so

[82] M. A. Mikkelsen: "The Bishop Hill Colony," p. 28 fl.

[83] For the facts in this paragraph see Emil Herlenius: "Erik-Jansismens Historia," p. 51; Eric Johnson and C. F. Peterson: "Svenskarne i Illinois," p. 28 and p. 233; and C. F. Peterson: "Ett Hundra Ar," p. 398.

[84] Eric Johnson: "Svenskarne i Illinois," pp. 28 and 29; Emil Herlenius: "Erik-Jansismens Historia," p. 60.

Sweden, whose pastors deceived the people by devilish doctrines, should through the Lord be destroyed with fire and sword by Eric Janson, the chosen prophet of God. And the Jansonists were eager to get away. Servants left their employers. "Wives fled from their husbands and babies." "Children deserted their homes and their parents."[85] They would be along with the rest to the land of promise.

In the new country "Eric Janson was to separate the children of God from the world and gather them into a theocratic community."[86] They expected no difficulty with the new language; for the prophet had promised that among whatsoever strange people they should come there should be given them at once power to speak their tongue. In the new country they were to eat wheat-bread and figs. The heathen were to build for them cities and walls. All were to be as one great family. The lion was to eat straw like the ox. Serpents and scorpions were not to harm the chosen people of God. They were now to have freedom unmolested to serve the Lord as they deemed right, and they would no longer be persecuted for trying to win others to their faith. The prophet was now to establish a New Jerusalem. And from this New Jerusalem was to radiate the true Christianity which was to convert America and from America was to spread to the ends of the earth. Then should come the Millennium. And in the Millenium, as the representative of Christ, Eric Janson or his descendants should rule till time is no more.[87]

PART THREE: THE BISHOP HILL COLONY.

I.

The Colony During Janson's Rule.

When the first shipload of Jansonists arrived, the prophet went from Victoria, Illinois, to meet them in New

[85] Emil Herlenius: "Erik-Jansismens Historia," pp. 51 and 61.
[86] M. A. Mikkelsen: "The Bishop Hill Colony," p. 25.
[87] The statements in this paragraph have been based upon Emil Herlenius: "Erik-Jansismens Historia," pp. 52 and 64; and upon M. A. Mikkelsen: "The Bishop Hill Colony," pp. 25 and 26.

York.[88] They went by steamboat up the Hudson River to Albany; thence to Buffalo by canalboat; and from Buffalo over the Great Lakes in "propellers" to Chicago.[89] A correspondent to a newspaper[90] tells of the impressions which the Jansonists, during their stay in Chicago, made upon him. He says: "I must write to you of an interesting band of immigrants, who have been encamped for the last three days under my windows. They are Swedes, in number about sixty-five, who have been obliged to leave their country by the most severe and constant persecution, on account of religious opinion. Their leader is Eric Eanson or Janson, an intelligent and strong-minded peasant, who has the most perfect confidence and control of the whole band. They look upon him as a sort of apostle, from a remarkable gift of second sight, which he certainly appears to possess. . . . There was a look about these people which I have never seen among the masses of European immigrants who have passed through Chicago since I have lived here. It was an expression of patient, intelligent endurance; all had it except the young children. They were not bowed down with weakness and care, like the French and Italian immigrants, not stern and stolid like the newly-arrived Germans, not wild and vehement like many of the Irish,—they walked erect and firm, looking always hopeful and contented, though very serious."—From Chicago most of the immigrants thus described walked all the way to Victoria —a distance of some one hundred miles. Horses and wagons, however, were provided for the children and for elderly persons.[91] The company arrived in Victoria in July, 1846. After a few days, they settled down near Red Oak Grove, three miles west from the future Bishop Hill. They began now to look about for a suitable location for a village, and they decided upon the southeast quarter of section 14, township 14, the same township in which was situated Red Oak Grove. This land was bought from the United States government on

[88] M. A. Mikkelsen: "The Bishop Hill Colony," p. 29.
[89] Emil Herlenius: "Erik-Jansismens Historia," p. 63.
[90] The Brook Farm "Harbinger." Quoted by William Alfred Hinds in "American Communities," p. 304.
[91] M. A. Mikkelsen: "The Bishop Hill Colony," p. 29; and Emil Herlenius: "Erik-Jansismens Historia," p. 63.

the 26th of September, 1846. The price paid for it was $200. Here, then, was built the village of Bishop Hill.[92]

In expectation of the other colonists, who were soon to follow, the Jansonists began with all the vigor they had to put up new dwellings. And not to forget a church. For they had come that they might worship God unhindered, and they must have a church. This so-called "church-tent" was built in the form of a cross, of logs and canvas. The entrance and the pulpit were in the north end; in the south end were a gallery and a large fire-place. The whole structure accommodated from eight hundred to a thousand persons. When the next company of Jansonists arrived, there were put up this church, two log houses, and four large tents.[93]

The second party of Jansonists—under the leadership of Jonas Olson—arrived on the 28th of October. Jan and Peter Janson, two brothers of the prophet, and their mother had also set out with this company, but the mother had died on the journey. In New York several had broken away from the party for the reason that, on account of the hard treatment and the great sufferings which they had undergone during the ocean voyage, they had begun to doubt the divine commission of their prophet. He had declared that upon their arrival in the new country, they should at once be able to talk the language of the land. They found now that they were not able to do so. How could a man who thus deceived them be a prophet sent by God? And many would no longer be numbered among the Jansonists. Some went along as far as to Chicago. Among those who remained in that city was Jan Janson, the brother of the prophet.[94]

Before the end of 1846, two more companies had arrived. The number of colonists now was about four hundred, of whom seventy lived at Red Oak Grove. To accommodate all these people, new dwellings were necessary. More log houses were hurriedly built, and there was put up a large sod-house which served as kitchen and dining hall. And the colonists

[92] Eric Johnson and C. F. Peterson: "Svenskarne i Illinois," p. 29 fl.
[93] Eric Johnson and C. F. Peterson: "Svenskarne i Illinois," p. 30.
[94] Emil Herlenius: "Erik-Jansismens Historia," p. 63 fl.

even resorted to "dug-outs." These were dug into the hillside, and were some twenty-five or thirty feet long and eighteen feet wide. Twelve of these "dug-outs" were made for the first winter, and each accommodated twenty-five or thirty persons. In one of them there lived fifty-two unmarried women.[95]

As if in favor to the Jansonists, the first winter was mostly very mild. The ground was frozen for only eight weeks. During that time, however, it was sometimes so cold that outside work had to be suspended.—Services were held three times on Sundays and two times on week-days. Eric Janson himself was up at five o'clock in the mornings, walking from hut to hut and calling the colonists to devotion. Half an hour later, he made the second round, and all were expected to appear promptly. Their devotional gatherings lasted often for two hours. About Christmas time a bell was procured, and Janson now used this instead of making his rounds.—The Jansonists did not neglect education; for several schools were established during this first winter. When the weather was such as to forbid outside work, instruction was given in the church-tent to adults, of whom many could not either read or write. A similar school was established in Red Oak Grove. About Christmas time an English school for children was begun in one of the dug-outs. The teacher was Mrs. Pollock. —One of the many difficulties which the colonists had to meet and conquer during this first winter was the procuring of sufficient flour. The nearest mill was twenty-eight miles away, and sometimes they had to go further. To help supply the wants, two hand-mills were made in which Indian corn was ground for porridge. To be eatable this porridge had to be cooked from ten to twelve hours. Sometimes the Jansonists would take turns and grind all night so as to provide meal for the coming day.[96] The prophet sought to remedy the want by announcing frequent fasts. If the people demurred, he would usually say: "You ought to be able to live on one-eighth less than you had in Sweden, if you had faith; but you are sick and

[95] Eric Johnson and C. F. Peterson: "Svenskarne i Illinois," p. 30 ff.
[96] Charles Nordhoff: "The Communistic Societies of the United States," p. 344.

die because you do not believe what I have prophesied."— The sanitary conditions in the dark and crowded houses were not of the best, and the climate was new to the colonists. Sickness of various kinds, mostly fever, ague, and diarrhœa, visited them, and many were those who succumbed. Sometimes seven or eight were brought to their last resting place on the same day. Some were buried in coffins, and some without. The prophet would allow no doctors; their faith should be their only cure; those who did not believe were worthy of no commiseration. Sickness was a proof that those who suffered did not believe Eric Janson whom God had sent to be a "propitiation for the people." Jonas Hedstrom, the Methodist preacher and brother of J. G. Hedstrom, threatened to report Janson to the proper authorities if he did not provide a doctor for the sick. And the prophet yielded. An American doctor was engaged, and, strangely enough, he was consulted even by Janson himself. Still, the opinion was long entertained that he who had faith needed no doctor, and those who employed one were long looked upon as being hard of belief. Under all these difficulties, there were some of the Jansonists who grew weary and left the colony. The prophet tried to prevent departures by stationing armed guards in the night. But most of the Jansonists were steadfast and bore up bravely; there was not a great deal of complaint among them; they looked forward to better things; some there were who even found heart to be happy.[97]

The Jansonists believed that they had in their possession the only true, saving doctrine, and that the world through them should be regenerated. In Eric Janson's Catechism there was the following assertion: "As the splendor of the second temple at Jerusalem far exceeded that of the first, erected by the son of David, so also the glory of the work which is to be accomplished by Eric Janson, standing in Christ's stead, shall far exceed that of the work accomplished by Jesus and his Apostles."[98] In order that this work might

[97] Eric Johnson and C. F. Peterson: "Svenskarne i Illinois," p. 31 fl. and p. 34. And Emil Herlenius: "Erik-Jansismens Historia," p. 70 fl.

[98] As given by M. A. Mikkelsen: "The Bishop Hill Colony," p. 25. See also p. 34.

be done, the prophet appointed twelve of the most gifted and promising young men in the colony to be apostles of his doctrine. As these men found that they did not through inspiration become masters of the English language, they sought to acquire it through study and practice, and they also studied Jansonistic dogmas. This was in 1847. They studied in the shade of a stately oak, and their teachers were some of the more advanced members of the colony.[99] After a few months of study, these twelve young men set out upon the task of converting the Americans and through them the world.

In this year, 1847, the Jansonists built a flour mill on the little creek running through the village. But the water was not always sufficient to drive the mill. "This new trouble was overcome in a manner both ingenious, simple, and practical; the health of the young theologians, the elders thought, might suffer by the effects of a too sedentary life, and to obviate this they were, at intervals between their studies, invited to step inside the wheel of the mill, and put this in motion by tramping at such occasions when the water supply was short in the creek.[100] After some time the mill was run instead by a horse.[101]

In the spring of 1847, the Jansonists began to prepare sun-dried brick, from which several substantial houses were built, some of which remained standing till 1862. In the summer of the following year the Jansonists learned to make also kiln-baked bricks. A saw-mill was set up at Red Oak Grove, but was soon traded away for a piece of land and another saw-mill, which was moved to the creek running through Bishop Hill. Roomy and convenient houses began to take the place of the dug-outs. And as the sanitary conditions improved, there was less sickness among the colonists.[102]

As time went on, more land was added to the colony. In November, 1847, a quarter section was bought for $380. Be-

[99] Eric Johnson and C. F. Peterson: "Svenskarne i Illinois," p. 32; and Emil Herlenius: "Erik-Jansismens Historia," p. 74 fl.

[100] John Swainson: "Swedish Colony at Bishops Hill, Illinois," found in O. N. Nelson: "History of Scandinavians and Biographies in U. S.," p. 144.

[101] Eric Johnson and C. F. Peterson: "Svenskarne i Illinois," p. 32.

[102] Ibid, p. 32 fl., and p. 35. Also Emil Herlenius: "Erik-Jansismens Historia," p. 72.

fore the end of 1847 the colonists had bought 359 acres in addition to the land already purchased. In May, 1848, eighty acres were bought for $1,500. Some of the colony land had been bought for as low as $1.25 an acre. For the last mentioned eighty, the colonists paid $18.75 an acre. Later Eric Janson himself bought not less than 10,116 acres.[103]

During the early hard times, outsiders sought to draw away the Jansonists from their leader and from their colony. A correspondent to Sweden states that the neighbors would come to the borders of the colony and exhibit their wheat-bread and other necessities of life and thus seek to prevail upon the Jansonists to leave their prophet. And the temptations were not only of a physical nature. Jonas Hedstrom was zealous in his attempts to win proselytes for Methodism. He even resorted to the spreading of discontent among the colonists. He sent men—perhaps those mentioned by the correspondent to Sweden—who pictured in beautiful colors the comforts to be had outside the colony; and the hardships of the Jansonists formed a dark background. And his work was by no means without result. In the fall of 1848, between two hundred and three hundred Jansonists left the colony and joined the Methodist church. But the majority remained steadfast. They entertained a remarkable devotion to their prophet. In a letter of 1847 or 1848 Janson is spoken of as "The lion of the tribe of Judah who has eyes like flames of fire and can see into our hearts and reveal all the thoughts of the heart." Correspondents of this period state that they have no thought of deserting Bishop Hill or the teachings of their prophet.[104]

On the 4th of June, 1847, the number of Jansonists in the young colony was about doubled. The new immigrants had suffered immensely on the journey. A person who renounced Jansonism and left the company in New York tells of the sufferings which they underwent in that city. They were crowded together in unhealthy rooms, and the food was unwholesome. Some suffered terribly from sickness. In four-

[103] Eric Johnson and C. F. Peterson: "Svenskarne i Illinois," p. 30, 33 fl.
[104] Ibid, p. 35; and Emil Herlenius: "Erik-Jansismens Historia," p. 71.

teen days, thirty of them died. The leaders were continually practising miraculous healing upon the unfortunate. One Jansonist was appointed minister to the sick. He preached two hours morning and evening, and he denounced roundly their unbelief on account of which they were sick. He declared that if they would throw all their sickness upon him, they should be well again, but if they could not, they should with the uncircumcised be thrown into hell for time and eternity. It was preached that as long as there was an Ackan among them, Israel could not conquer. Hence, in order to separate the hypocrites from the faithful, a fast was ordained which was to last for forty days. While the people were fasting the first day, one of the prophets went into the city and both ate and drank. This, he said, he could do in the surety of his faith. After the first day of fasting, many left the Jansonists, and the fast was broken; for it was judged that the hypocrites had now left.[105]

The sixth company of Jansonists came in 1849 under the leadership of Jonas Nylund. He had been to Norway and there persuaded a great number to join the colony. Between Chicago and La Grange they were attacked by the Asiatic cholera, and they brought with them the sickness to Bishop Hill. None of the Norwegians, however, died in the epidemic. It may further be stated that all of them—with the exception of three—left the colony to seek their fortune in other places.—The seventh party came in 1850. Between Buffalo and Milwaukee these were also attacked by the Asiatic cholera, and before the boat sailed in to the harbor at Milwaukee, fifty or sixty persons had been buried in Lake Michigan.—During the same year, another company arrived, consisting of about eighty Jansonists. And in 1854 came the last party, made up of seventy persons. This ended the mass-emmigration of the Jansonists. In addition to these nine large companies, there had come at times also individual persons. The entire number has been estimated at about one thousand,

---

[105] From O. S. Soderhamn: "Erik-Jansismen i Nord-amerika," p. 5 fl., as told by Herlenius in his "Erik-Jansismens Historia," p. 64 fl.

five hundred. One ship was lost at sea, and none of the fifty Jansonists were saved.[106]

It is interesting to know that Cleng Peerson, who has been called "The pathfinder of Norwegian immigration," was for a short time a member of the Bishop Hill Colony. When we have read the following quotation, it may not be out of the way to remember that this Peerson has been described as "restless, unstable, a lover of adventure, perhaps a victim of 'vanderlust.'" "In 1847 Cleng Peerson, now a man of sixty-five years, having sold his land in Missouri, joined the famous communistic settlement in Henry County, Illinois—the Swedish Bishop Hill Colony. He is reported to have contributed to this society the money which he had received from the sale of his farm lands. He now evidenced a purpose to settle permanently and to renounce his nomadic habits. His wife in Norway, from whom he had been separated since 1821, had died some years before Peerson arrived at the Bishop Hill Colony. He now married a young Swedish woman, a member of the communist settlement. His second marital venture seems to have been a short and bitter experience, for shortly after his marriage he departed from both the colony and his Swedish wife, and returned to the Fox River settlement. He is reported to have said that he left the Bishop Hill Colony 'robbed of all he possessed, and sick in body and mind.'"[107]

The Bishop Hill Colony was an ant-hill for diligence. All—men, women, children—had their work to do. From the flax crop of 1847 the Jansonists made 12,000 yards linen; from that of 1848, 12,454 yards and 4,120 yards of mats; from that of 1850—in which year they reached their height in the production of linen—28,322 yards of linen and 3,237 yards of mats.[108]—"Indian corn was planted for several years in the following manner: "Two men, walking in a straight line

---

[106] Emil Herlenius: "Erik-Jansismens Historia," p. 67 fl., and Eric Johnson and C. F. Peterson: "Svenskarne i Illinois," pp. 29, 33, 37, 38.

[107] From Theodore C. Blegen's article on Cleng Peerson in "The North Star," May-June, 1921, p. 218 and p. 213 fl. See also "The Mississippi Valley Historical Review," vol. VIII, no. 4, March, 1921, p. 323 and p. 328.

[108] Eric Johnson and C. F. Peterson: "Svenskarne i Illinois," p. 35 fl.

opposite each other, carried each a stake to which was fastened a rope stretched out and having a ribbon tied to it every four feet. Behind each ribbon walked a woman, who, with the help of a hoe, planted the corn she carried in an apron. After a time corn was planted in another manner: A 'marker' made of wood was driven over the prepared soil, and where the lines crossed girls dropped the kernels after which women, carrying hoes, covered up the seed. As the years passed by corn-planting machines made their appearance.''[109]—The small grain was cut, in 1847, with scythes. In 1848 cradles were taken into use. In order to get the cutting done in time, there were, in 1849, thirty persons at work night and day. In the same year a "reaper" was procured, but it worked so badly that it was sent back, and the cradles were again taken into use. And the Jansonists knew how to use the cradle. Two men are mentioned who each cut fourteen acres of wheat between sunrise and sunset. When the work was done, the grain cutters came marching home, "two by two, all in a line, with their peculiar cutting instruments on the shoulder, while after them came the women, likewise arranged in file, and at last the children, the whole army of cutters consisting of more than two hundred people and all singing some cheerful song.''[110]

During the first few years of colonial life, marriages were forbidden among the members. As a result, many Jansonists left the colony. The prophet then began to preach that he had received testimony to this effect: "The sons and daughters of Israel should enter wedlock, multiply themselves, and replenish the earth." The former prohibition was explained as being necessary "by reason of the distress" —as for instance lack of dwelling houses—which had been upon them in the early days. The restriction was removed in 1848. The command was now that all to whom God had given a desire to marry should forthwith be joined together or else be condemned to hell. Naturally, under such induce-

[109] Philip Stoneberg in Henry Kiner's "History of Henry County, Illinois," vol. 1, p. 635.

[110] Eric Johnson and C. F. Peterson: "Svenskarne i Illinois," p. 36.

ment on the one side and such prospects on the other, many married. "In fact, a number of young people were 'paired off' regardless of personal likes and dislikes. But as obedience had been a cardinal virtue so far, it was even in this." On one occasion "twenty-five couples were joined in wedlock" on one Sunday in the grove. "Each bride had the customary bridal wreath, the only personal adornment that was allowed." At another time, fourteen couples were married on the same day.[111]

In the summer of 1849 a great calamity befell the young colony. The sixth company of immigrants brought with them at that time the Asiatic cholera. The sickness broke out in the colony on the 22nd of July and raged till the middle of September. It happened that as many as twelve died in twenty-four hours. "Families fled temporarily from the colony, but death followed them; and in one instance a wife, miles distant from any assistance, buried her husband with her own hands.[112] Eric Janson fled with his family to a place near La Grange—about sixteen miles northwest from Bishop Hill—and when he had been there for some time, he ordered the colonists who were well to move thither also. They did so, but brought the sickness with them also to that place. Eric Janson with his family and some women now moved to an island in the Mississippi, where some Jansonist fishermen had been stationed. But the epidemic pursued them also to that place. The two youngest of their four children died here, and here died Janson's wife also. During the eight weeks through which the cholera lasted one hundred and forty-three colonists died, most of whom were young and middle-aged persons.[113]

Eric Janson was not only a religious leader; he was also the absolute ruler of temporal affairs in the colony. And he appears not to have been the shrewdest business man. When

[111] Philip J. Stoneberg in Henry Kiner's: "History of Henry County, Illinois." vol. 1, p. 637. And Emil Herlenius: "Erik-Jansismens Historia," p. 73 fl. See also G. Unonius: "Minnen," vol. 2, p. 376.

[112] William Alfred Hinds: "American Communities," p. 305.

[113] Eric Johnson and C. F. Peterson: "Svenskarne i Illinois," p. 37, and Emil Herlenius: "Erik-Jansismens Historia," p. 76.

it was decided to receive medical aid in the colony, one Robert D. Foster, who claimed to be a "botanical doctor," was recommended by Janson, voted upon, and elected. A quarrel broke out between Foster and a member of the colony, and Eric Janson requested the colonists to decide by a vote whether or not Foster should be discharged. This was done, and the doctor was ousted. Janson was provoked at this result, and a secret agreement was made between him and the doctor to the effect that the latter should be the family physician of Mr. Janson. It was claimed that the doctor was to have $2,000 a year salary, and that if any of the colonists sought his aid, he was to be paid for that service extra.—Foster had known how to win the complete confidence of the prophet, and he stirred up suspicion and hatred between Janson and members of the colony who attempted to warn their leader.—Some eighteen miles from Bishop Hill Foster owned 10,116 acres of land. First he sold Janson the wheat on the farm, and Janson, thinking there was more grain than was actually the case, paid too much for it. The harvesting and threshing of the grain had to be done by members of the colony, who received no remuneration for their work. Then Foster sold the land itself to Janson. The cash in the common treasury did not suffice to pay the debts in which the prophet was now involved. To meet his obligations, Janson gave up to Foster all the stock of the colony—"horses, oxen, cows, hogs, and calves." And not only all that but wagons, grain, bedclothes, food-supplies, and many other things. Under these privations the colony, of course, suffered. Eric Janson himself, however, kept a household of his own, and on his table was to be found the best of everything.[114]—When the trouble into which Janson had brought the colonists through his poor investments was at its height, Jonas Olson, Nils Hedin—one of the apostles,—and E. U. Norberg went to the prophet one day to remonstrate with him for wasting property which was common possession. The first two mentioned men, however, stood in such fear of their master that they did not dare to

[114] Emil Herlenius: "Erik-Jansismens Historia," p. 75 fl. See also G. Unonius: "Minnen," vol. 2, p. 380.

state their grievance, but instead intimated that Norberg was dissatisfied with Janson's management. Nettled at the falseness and cowardice of his two companions, Mr. Norberg decided to take upon himself the whole censure, and he gave the prophet a long admonition. He had long seen with sorrow, he said, how Eric Janson disregarded and treated harshly a people who for his teaching had renounced the faith of their fathers, had been persecuted and imprisoned, had suffered the loss of their property, had forsaken their fatherland, and had sustained untold suffering. The colonists had worked beyond their strength in order to promote the common welfare of all. Never had their views and opinions been consulted. Instead of treating them like friends and brothers he had treated them like slaves. His will had been a law with which none had the right to feel dissatisfied. To this remonstrance Janson replied: "I have acted according to my testimony; he who felt dissatisfaction therewith was deceived by the devil."[115]

When Eric Janson came back to La Grange after the death of his wife, he delivered a sermon in which he declared that the people had murdered their spiritual mother and his children by their unbelief. But, said he, at the death-bed of his wife there had been present a woman who had received upon herself the spirit of the departed, and who should at some future time exercise the same power as the one who had lately died.—Some days after, a sermon was delivered in which it was declared that Israel could not be rescued unless the prophet entered into a new wedlock. Though destruction had passed over Bishop Hill, there should be heard on the streets of Jerusalem the voice of bride and bridegroom. No weeping and sighing over departed spouses and children should be heard, but all should rejoice in the Lord.—About three weeks after Mrs. Janson's death, the prophet spoke again in a sermon about his wedding for the saving of Israel. All the Jansonists were to feel testimony in themselves as to who should be the spiritual mother, and she herself was like-

[115] Emil Herlenius: "Erik-Jansismens Historia," p. 77 fl.

wise to feel this testimony, and she should therefore come to Janson after the service and say that she was the one determined by God to occupy this office. There were two women who felt this testimony in their heart. One of them was Sophia Gabrielson, formerly Mrs. Pollock. The choice fell upon her; for she had the right testimony. She was now declared to be the spiritual mother of the Jansonists.—A week after, the wedding took place. It was celebrated in the private house of Mr. Janson. The bridegroom was cheerful and happy, but a cloud seemed to hang over his guests. The affair resembled more a funeral, said Janson, than it did a wedding.[116]

Sophia Pollock was a Swedish woman by birth, a daughter of a merchant in Goteborg. Her father went bankrupt, and she was taken as a foster-child by a well-to-do family, which later moved to New York. She was richly endowed as to abilities, and she was furthermore a beautiful woman. She was married in her young years to a seaman. He set out upon a voyage not long after, and he was never heard of again. After awhile she married one Mr. Pollock, the head of a private school in New York. Both accompanied Eric Janson to Victoria, and Mrs. Pollock, to the great sorrow of her husband, became a member of the colony. One writer says that Mr. Pollock died from grief, and that Mrs. Pollock took the affair so to heart that for a short time she lost her mind. She was next married to Lars Gabrielson, her third husband. Not long after the wedding, he fell a victim to the Asiatic cholera. And then she became Mrs. Janson. On the very day when she was designated the spiritual mother of the Jansonists, she undertook the management of the women's work in the colony. She also acted as secretary to her husband.[117]

As Eric Janson was ruler of the temporal affairs, so, of course, he was ruler of the religious life in the colony. The Jansonists met at times for services in a grove close to the

---

[116] From Emil Herlenius: "Erik-Jansismens Historia," p. 76 fl. About Janson's second marriage see also G. Unonius: "Minnen," vol. 2, p. 378 fl.

[117] Emil Herlenius: "Erik-Jansismens Historia," p. 77.

north of Bishop Hill. There were two meeting places in the grove. "It also happened that Janson sat on the porch of the frame house he occupied and preached to the people seated about. Janson, wearing a cloak of black, had direction of the services and frequently preached."[118] Some of the many other preachers were Jonas Olson, Anders Berglund, Nils Hedin. A man, who was not in sympathy with Janson, visited the colony one Sunday and heard the prophet preach. "He began," says the visitor, "to preach after his usual custom about his likeness to God, etc." When the visitor had been seated for a while and did not any longer desire to listen to what he considered unreasonable talk, he left the church. Janson, who understood that the man despised his doctrine, at once dropped the thread of his discourse and said: "There you see with your own eyes that the devil had to get out; for it is impossible for him to hear the Word of God preached in its purity."[119]—It is asserted that at one time the following incident took place at Bishop Hill: While the colonists were building a dam—and the weather evidently looked threatening—Eric Janson said: "If You, O God, do not give good weather so we can finish the work we have at hand, I shall depose You from Your seat of omnipotence, and You shall not reign either in heaven or on earth; for You can not reign without me."[120]—About the time when Janson permitted marriages in the colony—which he did in 1848—he also began to express himself less drastically in his sermons; and in his conversations with fellow countrymen who came to the colony he did not express any claims for himself except that he was an instrument in the hand of God to turn men back to live holy lives as had lived the early Christians. His writings were not shoved to the foreground. Outsiders were always approached carefully until by and by they were enmeshed. Only such things as could in reasonableness be

[118] Philip J. Stoneberg in Henry Kiner's: "History of Henry County, Illinois," vol. 1, p. 637.

[119] D. Londberg: "Nytt bref fran Amerika om Erik-Jansarnes tillstand derstades," p. 3-4, 6, as quoted by Emil Herlenius in "Erik-Jansismens Historia," p. 73.

[120] Emil Herlenius: "Erik-Jansismens Historia," p. 113, note 1.

accepted were presented as Jansonist doctrine.—At this time there came to the colony a man whose name was Johan Ruth, or, as he spelled it in this country, John Root. The necessity of having the true religion was impressed upon him.[121] John Root became a member of the colony.

John Root became a member of the colony in the autumn of 1848. He had been a sergeant in Sweden, had joined the United States army, and had served in the Mexican War. He was of a violent and revengeful nature. He married Charlotta Lovisa Janson, a cousin of the prophet. Open enmity soon broke out between Root and the master of Bishop Hill. A month after the marriage had taken place, Root desired to leave the colony with his wife. But at the wedding Janson had prevailed upon the bridegroom to sign a contract to the effect that if he left the colony, he should be divorced from his wife and let her remain. Root now, nevertheless, tried to persuade his wife to follow him. The prophet opposed her going, and she herself refused to go. For her soul's salvation she did not dare to leave; for the Jansonists were taught that if they forsook the teachings of the prophet or if they but left the colony, there was no salvation for them. Failing in his persuasive efforts, Root departed alone. He did not go far, however, but wandered about in the neighborhood, for a while serving as interpreter to a Jewish peddlar. The Jew suddenly disappeared, and Root was strongly suspected of having robbed and murdered the man. Some time after, the remains of a man were found under the floor of an outhouse.[122] After some months, Root returned to his wife, who in the meantime, had given birth to a son. She was still unwilling to leave with her husband. Incensed, Root threatened to kill Janson, and he swore at times that he would kill even his wife and child. He now decided to use force in bringing his wife away. He succeeded in getting her away from the colony, but alarm was sounded, and he was overtaken between two and three miles away. Mrs. Root came

[121] Emil Herlenius: "Erik-Jansismens Historia," p. 74.
[122] M. A. Mikkelsen: "The Bishop Hill Colony," p. 38 fl.

back to the colony. On the following day, Root served warrants on Janson and several others. The court was to be held in Cambridge. Mrs. Root was called in as witness, and she was brought from the colony without opposition. Root now brought his wife to some friends in the Rock River settlement. Mr. Janson declared that though it cost him half of Bishop Hill, she was to be returned to the colony. And finally she was returned. She remained there in secret so that only a few knew of her hiding place. When Root found himself deprived of his wife for the second time, his rage knew no bounds. He came to Bishop Hill with a force of about seventy men. He could find neither his wife nor Janson. The mob threatened that if Root's wife was not given to them inside of eight days, they would come back and burn the village. Eric Janson thought it best to leave Bishop Hill, and he went to St. Louis with his family and Mrs. Root. As revenge had been threatened also upon the men who had last brought Mrs. Root back to the colony, they were also afraid to remain, and therefore, with some others, set out for California to dig gold. For the "gold-fever" had reached the Jansonists also, and the colony was furthermore in a desperate condition financially. To make a long story short, Root failed to secure his wife. He swore on oath to the effect that he would take personal revenge upon Janson, and he sent word saying that he would shoot him at the first opportunity.[123]

Janson returned to the colony on the 11th of May, a Saturday. On the following day he preached his last sermon. The colonists have claimed unanimously that he was filled with evil forebodings. He applied to himself this passage from the Scriptures: "I am already being offered, and the time of my departure is come. I have fought the good fight, I have finished the course, I have kept the faith; henceforth there is laid up for me the crown of righteousness, which the Lord, the righteous Judge, shall give to me at that day; and

[123] This account and the following concerning Root and Janson I have built principally on Emil Herlenius: "Erik-Jansismens Historia," pp. 79-82. For a narrative concerning Root and Janson see also G. Unonius: "Minnen," vol. 2, p. 380 fl.

not to me only, but also to all them that have loved his appearing." It is also asserted that when he received the Lord's Supper on that same day, he quoted this passage: "I say unto you, I shall not drink henceforth of this fruit of the vine, until that day when I drink it new with you in my Father's kingdom."—On the following day, May 13th, 1850, he went to the court in Cambridge. At about one o'clock on that fatal day, after the court had adjourned for dinner, Eric Janson stood by a window in the courtroom, in conversation with a lawyer. Suddenly Root appeared outside the window. He asked Janson whether or not he would give back to him his wife and child. Janson made an insulting reply. A few moments afterward, Root stood in the door and called out Janson's name.[124] As the latter turned, Root fired his revolver. Janson fell on his back, pierced through the heart. He did not utter a word. A few moments, and he was dead. While the affair took place, the court-room was full of people.

Root was at once arrested. After a law-process of two years, he was sentenced to imprisonment for three years. After a year and a half, he was pardoned by Governor Matteson, who had received a great number of petitions for the release of the prisoner. Root went to Chicago. He was there strongly suspected of having played a part in the many robberies which at that time took place in the city. After some years he died in misery.

The death of Eric Janson spread consternation and deep sorrow in the colony. How had the mighty fallen in Israel? Was this the end of the man sent to be the representative of Christ on earth? Many of the colonists could scarcely believe it possible that he was dead. Some even thought: "Might not the same power that raised Jesus from the grave raise up Janson also? They wept and prayed and waited three days for the manifestation of resurrection power."[125] Then Eric Janson was buried. A simple wooden slab was

---

[124] Some have claimed that Root did not speak to Janson from outside the window, but that he suddenly appeared in the doorway, called Janson's name, and then fired.

[125] William Alfred Hinds: "American Communities," p. 309.

placed there to mark his resting place. Later a beautiful monument of white marble was raised to his memory.

II.

The Colony After Janson's Death.

According to a prophesy by Eric Janson, his son should, after the prophet's death, "sit on Moses' seat." But when Janson died, his son was not old enough to take the leadership in the colony. "The spiritual mother," therefore, placed herself at the head of affairs and selected as her assistant Anders Berglund. He was now, as he said, attired in "the mantle of Elijah," and, together with the prophet's wife, he soon held sway in the colony. He was regarded as standing in the place of the late Eric Janson until the prophet's son should reach a mature age.

Jonas Olson heard in California of Eric Janson's death. He decided at once to return to Bishop Hill, and he arrived in February, 1851. He deemed himself the logical man for the leadership of the colony after the prophet's death, but now Berglund held that position. Olson was cunning, careful, eloquent. He began secretly to undermine Berglund's authority. The imperiousness exerted over the colonists ought, said he, to be done away with. All should be brothers. True, Eric Janson had stood as the vicar of Christ, but this dignity had been given to him only. No man could inherit that high rank, for no other man could in the same measure get the Spirit of God. None should be master over the others; there should be equal rights for all; the spiritual mother was unnecessary. After having spoken in this wise privately to some of his most influential friends, Olson began, at first carefully, then more boldy, to preach the same principles publicly. The colonists began to see things from the same viewpoint. A struggle ensued between Olson and Berglund, each having their following, but Olson conquered along the whole line. Soon he had the confidence of all. A "democratic-republican" administration was inaugurated—a form of government entirely new in the colony. Persons were selected to stand at the head of the various activities. These men held frequent meetings and jointly decided on the affairs of the colony. In important cases, the opinion of the people was often consulted. Both their farming and their other industries began to prosper. In the summer of 1851, they began the cultivation of broom-corn, and this undertaking was found to pay handsomely. In the fall of the previous year, Olof Johnson, whom the prophet had sent to Sweden to collect some money due the Jansonists, had returned bringing with him some $6,000. The heaviest debts were now lifted from the colony; prosperity took the place of the late stringency; the future looked promising.[126]

But democracy did not last long in the colony. There were some who felt that they ought to have authority to rule without consulting the will of the common colonists. Among these men were Olof Johnson and Jonas Olson. At this time the latter was the most prominent man in the colony, and it may be said that he ruled affairs almost single-handed. Whether right or wrong, an author[127] makes this remark about him: "The result shows that under the mask of meekness he hid an uncommonly strong inclination to rule over others." He was more circumspect than the other men who aimed at winning authority. For some time, a number of people had realized the advisability of having the colony incorporated. Now Jonas Olson announced that a request for the incorporation of Bishop Hill should be sent to the State Legislature. The son of the founder says concerning this undertaking: "While nothing can be said against the desire to have the colony placed under the laws of the State, and although we do not have any reason to suspect of any evil those who undertook the work, still we can not forget to remark here that that charter was drawn up under a deep-laid plan which aimed to strengthen and perpetuate the power which certain persons already possessed. A more ingenious, crafty, and

[126] Emil Herlenius: "Erik-Jansismens Historia," pp. 83-84, and Eric Johnson and C. F. Peterson: "Svenskarne i Illinois," p. 38 and p. 41.
[127] Emil Herlenius.

dangerous instrument than this charter has never been adopted by the legislative assembly of this State.''[128] There were seven men mentioned in the charter who were to be trustees of the corporation. They were Olof Johnson, Jonas Olson, James Ericson, Jacob Jacobson, Jonas Kronberg, Swan Swanson, and Peter Johnson, a brother of the prophet. Five of them were related to each other. They were not elected by the people, but they let their names be written into the charter, and thus they appointed themselves to office. It was stipulated that ''The said Trustees and their successors in office may make contracts, purchase real estate, and again convey the same, whenever they shall see proper so to do for the benefit of the Colony.''[129] The proposed act was passed by the Legislature on the 17th of January, 1853. Bishop Hill was incorporated.

Being established in power, the trustees began a rule which could in no way be censured. The prosperity of Bishop Hill was greatly increased. All the land which had belonged to the colony under Eric Janson's rule, but which since had been sold to pay off debts, was now re-purchased, and other land was added. According to the report of the trustees in January, 1855, the colony owned 8,028 acres of land; 50 lots in Galva, valued at $10,000; railroad stock, valued at $1,000; 109 horses and mules; 586 cattle; 1,000 hogs; and wheat, flax, and broom-corn, and miscellaneous things, all valued at $37,471.02. The debts were $18,000.[130] One writer says about the Jansonists: ''They had the finest cattle in the state.''[131]

I will quote here a paragraph from ''The Practical Christian,'' year 1856:[132] ''There is at the present time a population of seven hundred and eighty in the community. They possess 8,500 acres of land, of which 3,250 are under cultivation. About 500 acres of their land is timbered. The prop-

[128] Eric Johnson and C. F. Peterson: "Svenskarne i Illinois," p. 43.
[129] Section 6 of the charter.
[130] Emil Herlenius: "Erik-Jansismens Historia," p. 87. See also Eric Johnson and C. F. Peterson: "Svenskarne i Illinois," p. 44. The latter has $49,570 instead of $37,471.02.
[131] Charles Nordhoff: "The Communistic Societies of the United States."
[132] As given in William Alfred Hinds: "American Communities," p. 313 fl.

erty is held by seven trustees for the Community. They own some of the largest and best buildings in the country. They have two large unitary dwellings, one a 4-story brick building, 200 feet long, and 45 feet wide; the other a 3-story brick, 55 by 65 feet. They have also three or four more unitary dwellings, not so large; also a good mill, a tavern, some extensive shops and stores, one at the Community, and one at Galva, four miles off on the railroad. They own also a brick warehouse at Galva, 40 feet by 100, and likewise a large number of town-lots. They have over 200 milk cows, with as many calves, 150 head of horses and mules, 50 yoke of work oxen, and a stock of 600 additional head of cattle. They made about $36,000 out of their crop of broom-corn alone in 1854. It is said they intend taking stock in the Rock Island and Peoria Railroad to the amount of $150,000 or $200,000, if it runs near their village. The fact is they are rich."

A word here as to their communism: Families lived in separate rooms; they had separate beds, clothing, and other commodities. A large building was used as a common kitchen and dining hall, and the members all had their meals there at the same time. The women sat around two long tables and the men around one; for about two-thirds of the members of the colony were women.[133] All were given their necessary clothing. The by-laws of 1854 have this to say concerning the property of the colonists: "The property which any person on becoming a member of this Colony shall transfer to the trustees thereof, shall become forever thereafter the absolute property of the Colony; and on withdrawal or discontinuance of membership by any person, he shall not be entitled to compensation or pay for any service or labor he may have performed during the time he may have been a member; but it shall be at the option of the trustees to give to such person such things, whether money or property, as they, the trustees, shall deem right or proper."

A man[134] who visited Bishop Hill in 1853 writes this paragraph about the colony: "We had occasion this year to visit

[133] M. A. Mikkelsen: "The Bishop Hill Colony," p. 53.

[134] John Swanson in "Swedish Colony at Bishopshill, Illinois," in O. N. Nelson's "History of Scandinavian and Biographies in United States," p. 149 fl.

the colony, and were received with the greatest kindness and hospitality. Everything, seemingly, was on the top of prosperity. The people lived in large substantial brick houses. We had never before seen so large a farm, nor one so well cultivated. One of the trustees took us to an adjacent hill, from which we had in view the colony's cultivated fields, stretching away for miles. In one place we noticed fifty young men with the same number of horses and plows cultivating a corn field, where every furrow was two miles in length. They moved with the regularity of soldiers. In another part was a field of a thousand acres broom corn, the product of which, when baled, was to be delivered to Boston parties at Peoria, and was supposed to yield an income of fifty thousand dollars. All their live stock was exceptionally fine, and apparently given the best care. There was a stable of more than one hundred horses, the equals of which would be hard to find. One evening I was brought to an enclosure on the prairie, where the cows were milked. There must have been at least two hundred of them, and the milkmaids numbered forty or fifty. There was a large wagon, in which an immense tub was suspended on four posts, and in this each girl, ascending to the top by a step-ladder, emptied her pail. The whole process was over in half an hour. On Sunday I attended service. There was singing and prayer, and the sermon, by one of the leaders, contained nothing that a member of any Christian denomination might not hear in his own church. Altogether, I retained the most agreeable remembrance of this visit."

The chief preacher in the colony at this time was Jonas Olson. He was assisted by Anders Berglund, Nils Hedin, and Olof Asberg. Any male member of the colony, however, had the privilege of preaching if he desired. Strangers who visited their church were impressed by their beautiful singing. It was preached that all worldly affairs should be subordinate to the religious idea upon which the colony was founded and which bound together the members. The sharpest corners of Jansonism were by this time worn off, and their religion was now much like that of the former moderate religionists in Sweden, or like Methodism. The catechism composed by Eric Janson went gradually out of use, and his hymn book underwent a wholesome revision.—An English and a Swedish school were in operation. Reading, writing, and arithmetic were taught, and also a little in a few other subjects, but higher education was considered a dangerous thing which only served "to puff men up." In 1860 a large school building was constructed—the last building to be put up by the colony.[135]—Newspapers were not allowed at Bishop Hill. Nor the reading of secular books except the text-books used in school. The Bible was considered sufficient reading for anyone. Nevertheless, a newspaper, "Den Svenska Republikanen i Norra Amerika," was established by the Jansonists in Galva in 1856, but it was of short duration.[136]

As the colony prospered, pride and selfishness began to grow strong in some of the trustees—particularly in Olof Johnson and Jonas Olson. The latter was looked upon as being both the secular and the religious leader of the colony. He was not averse to be titled "king," and the other trustees were frequently styled "princes." As their aspirations to eminence grew, their disregard for the will of the people also increased. Large contracts were signed and great speculations were entered into without the knowledge of the people. Olof Johnson and Jonas Olson were often the only ones who knew of the undertakings. If someone became inquisitive as to the affairs of the colony, he was likely to receive a sharp reprimand for his suspicions against the management. Such a one had "Martha's anxiety about many things, but lacked the spirit of the apostle who exhorted each and all to pay heed in stillness to his own calling."[137]

The name of Nils Hedin has before been mentioned in this narrative. He was one of the twelve apostles appointed by Eric Janson to spread the only-saving teachings of the

---

[135] F. H. Wistrand: "Colonien Bishop Hill," referred to by Emil Herlenius: "Erik-Jansismens Historia," p. 89.

[136] Emil Herlenius: "Erik-Jansismens Historia," pp. 88, 89. See also A. C. Cole: "The Era of the Civil War," p. 150, note.

[137] Emil Herlenius: "Erik-Jansismens Historia," p. 89.

prophet among the people of the United States. This man was now to introduce a doctrine which became one of the greatest factors in dissolving the colony. In 1854 he visited the Shakers in Pleasant Hill, Kentucky, and through them he became convinced that celibacy had great advantages and was best in harmony with a true Christian life. Jonas Olson stumbled on this thing also. He began, together with the other leading preachers in the colony, to set forth "as a doctrine of the Bible that the marriage relation was an unchristian relation; that the relation belonged only to those who belonged under the law of Moses and to the heathens, but was condemnatory to true Christians. On this ground the marriage was not only forbidden those who wanted to become Christians in this scriptural sense, but those that were already married could no longer continue in the natural generation as they truly would fall from the grace of God."[138] "It was contrary to the will of God that husband and wife should live together as such."[139] "Natural generation was only the will of devil, to multiply the fallen human race."[140] According to the prophet Isaiah "thy sons shall come from far," said Olson, "and thy daughters shall be carried in the arms." Another reason for celibacy, said the preachers of Bishop Hill, was this: If the young women should marry, they could not perform their work out-doors, such as they customarily did in the brick-yard, in the stables, in the hog-yard, and on the fields.[141] In short, "the spiritual rulers of the Bishop Hill Colony permitted the married to live together, but not to exercise conjugal relations."[142] And the young people were not allowed to marry at all.

Great misery was brought about among the Jansonists through this diabolical doctrine of celibacy.—One couple, Eric Svenson and Britta Svenson, had been led to believe through

[138] From an affidavit by Anders Shogren, a member of the colony, given in Emil Herlenius: "Erik-Jansismens Historia," p. 131 fl.
[139] From a statement made by Jonas Westlund, a member of the colony. Quoted in Herlenius, p. 133.
[140] From an "appeal" signed by 41 persons from Bishop Hill. Quoted by Herlenius, p. 90.
[141] From the affidavit by Anders Shogren. Other facts in this paragraph are taken from Emil Herlenius: "Erik-Jansismens Historia," p. 90.
[142] Eric Johnson and C. F. Peterson: "Svenskarne i Illinois," p. 46 fl.

the preaching of Jonas Olson and the other demagogues that they ought to be divorced. Their three boys were left in the care of Mrs. Svenson. After Mr. Svenson had signed the divorce paper, he left Bishop Hill and lived in various places for about a year. He began, however, to regret his divorce. He blamed Jonas Olson as having in particular led him to take the hasty step, and he sent him a threatening letter in which he asked whose wife Britta Svenson was to be in the future, his own or Olson's. Fearing a fate like the one which had overtaken the late prophet, Jonas Olson devised a plan that should prevent all extremes. Mrs. Svenson was sent to her husband after being first carefully instructed as to how she ought to make her visit as unbearable as possible. Formerly the couple had lived together in harmony and happiness, but now she began to act in the most aggravating manner. And violent scenes resulted. Olson's plan was found to work. Mr. Svenson at last tired of contending with a wife who before had been dear to him, but who now had become his most bitter enemy. He moved to Kentucky, where he joined the Shakers, and his wife was again received at Bishop Hill, not, however, until the preachers had spread rumors as to how Svenson had lived in disharmony with his wife and how he had at last deserted her and the children and had left them destitute.—Another instance: A woman, Anna Hanson, desired to join the colony, but her husband opposed. Jonas Olson and Anders Berglund then instructed her how to proceed: She ought to deny her husband all conjugal relationship and in everything act obstinately toward him; the result would be that he at last would seek a divorce, and she would be free to join the colony. Mr. Hanson soon discovered whence the wind was blowing. He went to Bishop Hill and found Jonas Olson alone in a room. He requested to know what kind of talk Olson had been engaged in with Mrs. Hanson, and, adding that he would now teach him the consequences of mixing into the affairs of married people, he drew a revolver and pointed it at Olson's forehead. The shouts of the latter called together a crowd, and Hanson was arrested. It was found, however, that the revolver was not loaded.—

Only one more instance to show what havoc this celibacy doctrine wrought in many homes: One Jonas Westlund was persuaded by Olson and one of the other preachers that he ought to leave his wife. When the couple was living apart, Olson said one day to the husband: "It is best you take care of your child, because your wife is from her senses." In a statement concerning this affair, Mr. Westlund says further: "My wife called me to her and asked: 'Why can we not live together as husband and wife?' I answered: 'You know yourself, that this has happened, because we have concluded to obey. I have not done it in accordance with my own decree, but Olson has been my adviser.'—My wife did not thereafter speak with me for a long time. Last summer she took a razor and went to a desolate place and cut her throat,—as it seems with intention to end her life."[143]

When the leaders in the colony had been fully established for a while in their oligarchical power, some of them—and in particular Olof Johnson—began to indulge in far-reaching speculations. In 1853 a new village, Galva, was founded five miles from Bishop Hill. The Chicago, Burlington and Quincy railroad touched the new village, and the little station grew rapidly. Olof Johnson, on behalf of the colony, established various industries in the new town. In the beginning he was eminently successful. Before long he ruled practically single-handed, from his office in Galva, all the business affairs of the colony. As he prospered, he became presumptuous. He entered into the pork-packing business, into banking, into the grain brokerage business, into coal mining, into railroad affairs. Together with some others, he made a contract to build for $5,000,000 "The Western Air-Line Railroad," and on behalf of Bishop Hill he bought stock to the amount of one million dollars. When the financial depression struck this country in 1857, Bishop Hill suffered one big loss after the other. The two following years brought still further losses. Hard times thwarted every effort at building up new business ventures. The people demanded that some

[143] Westlund's statement is given in full in Emil Herlenius: "Erik-Jansismens Historia," p. 133 fl. The other incidents are told in the same book, pp. 92-94.

control should be exercised over the activities of the leaders, but the latter would in no wise have their powers clipped. In 1859 it became known that in order to cover losses the trustees had borrowed large sums of money. The colony demanded that the trustees should lay bare the true facts in the case. Several of the trustees answered that they knew nothing of this business, for Olof Johnson managed such affairs alone. Mr. Johnson refused absolutely to give any account. He admitted to have borrowed $50,000, but it was a private affair, he said, and the colony had no business to interfere in the matter. The only one of the trustees who seemed willing to have the colonists exercise some control over the leaders was Peter Janson, the brother of the late prophet, and he was replaced as a trustee by Olof Stenberg.—The deplorable business affairs began to point toward the dissolution of the Bishop Hill communism.[144]

And there were other things that pointed in the same direction. About 1859 the colonists "discovered that their young people, who had grown up in the society, were discontented, found the community life dull, did not care for the religious views of the society, and were ready to break up the organization."[145] One writer[146] says: "But had the financial interests of the Community been rightly managed it could not have existed much longer, in the opinion of many intelligent members, on account of the increasing difficulties experienced with their young people, who, as they grew up and learned something of the world around them, demanded greater freedom in amusement, more varied development, more liberty of thought and action, and more to do with the management of the colony's affairs. These very aspirations were to the older members evidences of the working of evil influences; and they met them, we will charitably believe, with all the wisdom and grace at their command; but still they failed—failed on the one hand to inspire their youth with their own religious fervor, and on the other hand to give them legitimate

[144] Emil Herlenius: "Erik-Jansismens Historia," p. 97 fl.
[145] Charles Nordhoff: "The Communistic Societies of the United States," p. 347.
[146] William Alfred Hinds in his book "American Communities," p. 318 fl.

freedom and scope. Large numbers of them left the colony for the outside world. This wrung the hearts of the fathers and mothers. It was torture for them to see their children go out without means, and without their own religious faith—besides their going drained the colony of its most vigorous life. 'We saw it could not go on so,' the venerable Berglund said to me."

The dissolution of the Bishop Hill communism began in 1860, and was completed during the two following years. "It was determined in the spring of 1860 to divide the property, the Olson party, as it was called, including two thirds of the members, determined with their share to continue the community, while the Janson party determined on individual effort. Hereupon two-thirds of the real and personal property was set apart for the Olson party, but for a whole year the two parties lived together at Bishop Hill. In 1861 the Janson party divided their share among the families composing it; and in the same year the disorganization proceeded another step. The Olson party fell into three divisions. In 1862, finally, all the property was divided:"[147] The communism of Bishop Hill had ceased to exist.

But the financial troubles of the colonists were not yet ended. "Property to the value of $592,798 was divided among 415 shareholders. The remainder of the property, according to the statement of 1860, amounting to $248,861, was put in the hands of the old trustees to pay the accrued debt of $118,-403.33, and five years time given them to effect the liquidation; but it being soon apparent that the sum thus put aside for paying the debt was not sufficient, on account of a number of worthless items, a further amount of $52,762 was delivered to the trustees by the colonists. At the expiration of five years the trustees informed the people that $100,000 were still needed to pay the debt, and actually collected in cash $56,153.71. Time rolled on. The trustees never gave any statement about payment of the debt, but instead of this, in the beginning of the year 1868, came notice that a still larger

[147] Charles Nordhoff: "The Communistic Societies of the United States," p. 347 fl.

amount was required to settle the obligations of the colony. This brought matters to a crisis. Forbearance ceased to be a virtue. The unfortunate colonists appointed a committee to wait upon the trustees and demand an account, and the latter flatly refused anything of the kind, litigation[148] commenced, which lasted five years, when a verdict was given by which the colonists were made to pay $57,782.90, of which amount $46,-290 were expenses for the suit and lawyers' fees. Besides this the colonists during the litigation assumed responsibility for the whole of the old colony debt with interest amounting to $158,000 minus the amounts paid in between the years 1860-1868. Thus, to pay a debt in 1860 of $118,401.33, these ill-fated people have actually expended in cash $413,124.61, and in property $259,786, or in the aggregate $672,910.61. This seems absurd and incredible, but the above are all official figures.''[149]

The Jansonists, unlike many small sects, were not opposed to war. ''In 1861 the community raised a company of soldiers for the Union army, furnishing both privates and officers.''[150] They fought through the war, and after the war one of them was admitted to West Point ''for meritorious conduct and promising intellect.'' He graduated with honor.

A writer[151] on Bishop Hill, whose book was published in 1857, says this about the old colony: ''At present Bishop Hill is slowly falling into decay. The houses are still mostly inhabited; there are several shops and stores; but the large buildings are out of repair; and business has centered at Galva, five or six miles distant. Most of the former communists live happily on their small farm.''—And Eric Johnson, the son of the founder of Bishop Hill, says in his book, published in 1880: ''It may truly be said that the general morals are nowhere better than in and around Bishop Hill,

[148] For an account of this law process see Eric Johnson and C. F. Peterson: "Svenskarne i Illinois," pp. 50-52. Herlenius refers also to "The Illinois Swede," 1869, no. 29, and 1870, nos. 12, 13, 19, 28.

[149] John Swainson: "Swedish Colony at Bishopshill, Illinois," p. 151 fl. in O. N. Nelson: "History of the Scandinavians and Successful Scandinavians in the United States."

[150] Charles Nordhoff: "The Communistic Societies of the United States," p. 348.

[151] Charles Nordhoff: "The Communistic Societies of the United States," p. 348 fl.

whose populace is particularly distinguished for strict sobriety, peaceableness, and industry."

PART FOUR: CONCLUDING REMARKS

The fiftieth anniversary of the founding of the Bishop Hill Colony was celebrated on September 23rd and 24th, 1896. "Over two thousand people were in attendance, among whom were no less than ninety-nine of the incorporators of 1853. Of the trustees two were living, Jonas Olson, aged ninety-four, and Swan Swanson.[152] From the first immigration there were also two living: Peter Johnson and Lars Erikson. Speeches were given by Captain Eric Johnson, the son of the founder; by Lawyer John Root, son of Eric Johnson's cousin and of the man who shot the prophet; and by Hon. J. W. Olson, son of the Olof Olson who came to prospect for the intended colony. A monument, a single large shaft of granite, was unveiled, bearing the following inscription:

1846

Dedicated to the Memory of the Hardy Pioneers

who, in order to secure

Religious Liberty

left Sweden, their native land, with all the endearments

of home and kindred, and founded

Bishop Hill Colony,

on the uninhabited prairies of

Illinois

Erected by surviving members and descendants

on the 50th Anniversary, September twenty-third

1896

[152] E. W. Olson: "History of the Swedes of Illinois," vol. 1, p. 266.

A parting word now on some of the chief actors in the play.—Sophia Janson, the widow of the prophet, received eleven acres as her share of the land when the property of Bishop Hill was divided. For a while she lived with the Shakers in Kentucky. Later she conducted a boarding house in Galva. She died in the Henry County infirmary in 1888. "She was buried beside her distinguished husband, near the center of the village cemetery, a few steps from a large cottonwood tree."—Eric Johnson, the son of the founder, joined Company "D" of the Illinois 57th infantry regiment in September, 1861. In April, 1862, he became lieutenant, and in September of the same year, captain. For a while he published the "Galva Union." In 1870 he received a majority of 2,000 votes for election to the legislature, but he had to renounce the honor for the reason that, according to the constitution, he had not lived long enough in the district. A writer whose book was published in 1908 says: "Eric Janson's son, Captain Eric Johnson, is now living in California, and the daughter, who was married to Captain A. G. Warner, a veteran of the Civil War, and later became Mrs. Rutherford, also survives."[153]—Olof Johnson, the trustee, died suddenly, without previous illness, on the 18th of July, 1870.—Mrs. John Root, with her child, remained at Bishop Hill.[154]—Eric Bergland, a son of one of the preachers at Bishop Hill, married Lucy Scott McFarland, a cousin of Mrs. Hayes, the wife of the President of the United States.—Sophia Schon returned to Sweden in 1868, or thereabouts.—Olof Olson, the prospector, never joined the community, but settled on a farm near Victoria. He and his wife and two of their children died in 1846, all inside of a few weeks.—Jonas Olson lived through nearly the whole of the 19th century. His wife died in 1871, and in the following year, Olson, then seventy years old, married a girl of twenty-eight. In his old age he became confined to a rolling-chair. He died at Bishop Hill on the 18th of November, 1898, then ninety-six years old.—"At the present time," says a writer[155] whose book was published

[153] E. W. Olson: "History of the Swedes of Illinois," vol. 1, p. 268.
[154] G. Unonius: "Minnen," vol. 2, p. 383.
[155] E. W. Olson: "History of the Swedes of Illinois," vol. 1, p. 268.

in 1908, "Bishop Hill is a small village with a population somewhat in excess of three hundred. The large buildings erected at the time of its greatest prosperity are still occupied, though somewhat dilapidated. But few of the early colonists now remain alive. Bergland, Norberg, Hedin, Stoneberg, Olof Johnson, and Jonas Olson, all the leaders have passed away and the second generation sprung from them and their contemporaries is already growing old.[156] In 1920 the population of Bishop Hill was two hundred and seventy-four. There was at that time a telegraph station and a money order post office.[157]

In the story of the Jansonists and the Bishop Hill colony we have it pointed out to us—as we have so often had it pointed out in similar ventures—that, as long as the human heart is what it is today, selfish and sinful, communism cannot for long endure. It has been tried so often and failed so often since it first was tried and first failed in the days of the Apostles. If the human heart had been free from selfishness, communism would perhaps have been the prevailing order among all men. Robert Owen held the belief that the human heart is in reality good, and upon this belief he founded his communistic societies. "He affirmed that 'human nature is radically good, and is capable of being trained, educated and placed from birth in such a manner that all ultimately must become united, good, wise, healthy and happy.' "[158] But Robert Owen failed; for human nature is not "radically good." He said himself that "he wanted honesty of purpose, and he got dishonesty. He wanted temperance, and instead he was continually troubled with the intemperate. He wanted industry, and he found idleness. He wanted cleanliness, and found dirt. He wanted carefulness, and found waste. He wanted to find desire for knowledge, but he found apathy. He wanted the principles of the formation of character understood, and he found them misunderstood. He wanted these

[156] For other facts in this paragraph see Eric Johnson and C. F. Peterson: "Svenskarne i Illinois," pp. 298, 302, 27, and Emil Herlenius: "Erik-Jansismens Historia," pp. 100, 63.

[157] Rand McNally: "Commercial Atlas of America," Chicago, 1921.

[158] As quoted in William Alfred Hinds: "American Communities," p. 128.

good qualities combined in one and all the individuals of the Community, but he could not find them, neither could he find those who were self-sacrificing and enduring enough to prepare and educate their children to possess these qualities.''[159] Not until ''the wolf shall dwell with the lamb, and the leopard shall lie down with the kid'' can communism live among us. When ''the earth shall be full of the knowledge of Jehovah, as the waters cover the sea,'' we may have communism.

The history of the Bishop Hill colony shows also this fact: When men once adopt some new fangled religion, they are prone to become unstable religiously. If they once are torn loose from the moorings of their childhood religion, they often drift like rudderless boats now with one wind and now with another, or they may be beaten to pieces at last upon the shoals of complete indifference to all religious beliefs. If they are Methodists today and become ''Pillars of Fire'' tomorrow, they may become Christian Scientists next week; or they may conclude that they will belong to no religious denomination whatsoever. So it was with the Jansonists. They had been brought up as Lutherans. Then they were led to burn their religious books and to take up the doctrine of a new prophet. When they had been Jansonists for a while, a great number of them became Methodists. Once, more than two hundred stepped over into that camp. Anders Berglund, once a leader among the Jansonists, became finally one of the preachers for a Methodist congregation.—Some of the Jansonists became Second Adventists. In 1870 a congregation was formed consisting of one hundred and fifty members. And here Jonas Olson stepped in. He had been a Lutheran, then a Jansonist, now a Second Adventist. At first he saw nothing wrong in marriage; then he advocated celibacy; then, a year after his wife's death, he married again.—Some of the Jansonists became Shakers. Ten colonists left Bishop Hill for Pleasant Hill, the Shaker colony in Kentucky. Nils Hedin, one of the twelve apostles, caught the celibacy doctrine from these Shakers. The ''spiritual mother'' of the

[159] William Alfred Hinds' American Communities, p. 35 fl.

Jansonists had been a Lutheran in her childhood; then she became the wife of the prophet of Jansonism; and then a member of the Shaker colony in Kentucky.—Some of the Jansonists became Swedenborgians.—And a great number of Jansonists became such as would belong to no religious denomination. Eric Johnson, the son of the founder, says in his book: "The majority of those who now dwell in this colony, so ultra-religious in the beginning, are outside of all congregations. . . . That they are highly indifferent with respect to theological dogmas is not surprising when one remembers what chaos has reigned in this respect and how many schools they have gone through without finding anything for them reliable." Religiously, the Jansonists were spread to all winds. They became a flock without a shepherd.—Jansonism was a house upon which the rain descended and the winds blew; and the house fell, for it was not founded upon the rock.

BIBLIOGRAPHY.

Eric Johnson and C. F. Peterson: "Svenskarne i Illinois." Chicago, 1880. "It is the oldest, and among the best authorities on the Swedish settlement at Bishop Hill."—O. N. Nelson. It contains a chapter on Henry County, thirty-three pages on the Bishop Hill Colony, and short biographies of some of the Jansonists. The article on Bishop Hill is written by Eric Johnson, the son of the founder. He has passed by many unpleasant features in silence.

G. Unonius: "Minnen fran en sjuttonarig vistelse i Nordvestra Amerika." Upsala, 1861-62. In two volumes. Volume two contains some pages on the Bishop Hill Colony. The author is a hostile critic of the Jansonistic movement.

O. N. Nelson: "History of the Scandinavians and Successful Scandinavians in the United States." Minneapolis, 1893. Contains article entitled: "Swedish Colony at Bishopshill, Illinois," written by Major John Swainson. The article was published in "Scandinavia" in 1884. It is favorable to Jansonism.

E. Norelius: "De svensk-lutherska forsamlingarnes och Svenskarnes historia i Amerika." Rock Island, 1890. Chapter three contains an article written by Harald Wieselgren in "Biografiskt Lexicon ofver namnkunnige svenske man." It contains also much from Eric Johnson's article in "Svenskarne i Illinois."

M. A. Mikkelsen: "The Bishop Hill Colony." Published in Johns Hopkins University Studies, January, 1892. He says: "Much of the information contained in this volume has needs been gathered from the lips of surviving members of the Bishop Hill colony." He acknowledges indebtedness to Jonas Olson, then in his 88th year, but "remarkably well preserved." The article is on the whole favorable to the Jansonistic movement.

Henry L. Kiner. "History of Henry County, Illinois." Chicago, 1910. In two large volumes. The article on the Bishop Hill Colony is written by Philip J. Stoneberg. He says: "Much information has been obtained from conversing or corresponding with old settlers."

Charles Nordhoff: "The Communistic Societies of the United States." New York, 1875. A good short summary of the social and economic side of the Bishop Hill Colony. He writes from personal visits and observations.

E. W. Olson and Martin Engberg, editors: "History of the Swedes of Illinois." Chicago, 1908. In two large volumes. Volume one contains a long and very good article on the Bishop Hill Colony, with pictures of buildings and of some prominent Jansonists.

William Alfred Hinds: "American Communities." Revised edition. Chicago, 1902. Contains twenty-one pages on Janson and the Bishop Hill Colony. Janson is shown mostly with his Sunday clothes on. The author does not seem to have been acquainted with the most complete history of the colony —that by Herlenius.

C. A. Cornelius: "Svenske kyrkans historia efter Reformationen." Upsala, 1886-87. In two volumes. Volume two contains about seven pages on Janson and the Bishop Hill Colony.

Emil Herlenius: "Erik-Jansismen i Sverige." Upsala, 1897. As the name indicates, this book treats mostly of the Jansonist movement in Sweden.

Emil Herlenius: "Erik-Jansismens Historia." Jonkoping, 1900. This book treats of the movement in Sweden and also of the Bishop Hill Colony. The author has had access to many newspapers printed in Sweden and to a great number of unprinted sources. Among the latter are: "Soderala Kyrkorads Protokoll," 1844-45; "Forssa Tingslags Domboker," 1845; "Helsinglands Norra Kontrakts Arkiv;" "Vesteras cellfangelses journal," 1844; "Erik Jansons egen lefnadsbeskrifning," (till 1844); Jonas Olson: "Om Jansonisternas forfoljelser i Sverige;" "En samling bref fran Bishop Hill;" E. N. Norberg: "Berattelse om Bishop Hill;" and J. E. Ekblom: "Laseriet i Osterunda och Erik-Jansonisterna under aren 1843-46." This book by Herlenius, "Erik-Jansismens Historia," is the most complete history of Eric Janson and the Bishop Hill Colony published to date. Pages 116-138 contain various documents, among which are "The Charter of the Bishop Hill Colony," "Statements made by Anders Shogren, member of the Bishop Hill Colony in Henry County," "The Old By-Laws of the Bishop Hill Colony," and "Statement, made by Jonas Westlund, concerning him and his wife, both members of the Bishop Hill Colony in Henry County."

A. C. Cole: "The Era of the Civil War." In "The Centennial History of Illinois," vol. 3. References are made to the Bishop Hill Colony on pp. 20, 21, 150, 341.

S. P. Orth: "Our Foreigners." This author has a few pages on the Colony.

C. F. Peterson: "Ett hundra Ar. En Atterblick paa det Nittonde Seklet." He has only a passing remark about Janson and his colony.

C. F. Peterson: "Sverige i Amerika." Chicago, 1898. He has a few pages, 19-22, devoted to Eric Janson, and a chapter on Jonas Olson, pp. 25-27.

John Wordsworth: "The National Church of Sweden." London, 1911. Lecture VII treats of "The Time of Freedom and the Period of Neology" in the church of Sweden, and lecture VIII treats of "The Modern Period." He devotes less than a page to Eric Janson and his movement.

Rand McNally: "Commercial Atlas of America." Chicago, 1921.

"The Mississippi Valley Historical Review," Vol. VII, No. 4, March, 1921. Contains an article by Theodore C. Blegen entitled "Cleng Peerson and Norwegian Immigration." The article mentions Mr. Peerson's connection with the Bishop Hill Colony.

"The North Star." A bi-monthly journal published by K. C. Holter Publishing Company, 416 8th Ave. So., Minneapolis. Volume 3, May and June, 1921, contains an article by Theodore C. Blegen: "Cleng Peerson, the Pathfinder of Norwegian Immigration."

"Svenska Tribunen." 28: de Arg., No. 40, Sept. 30, 1896. This issue has an article on the 50th anniversary of the founding of Bishop Hill, with a picture of Jonas Olson, one of the monument unveiled during the festivities, and several pictures of buildings at Bishop Hill.

"Hemlandet, Det Gamla och Det Nya." Chicago, Vol. 10, No. 283, June 8, 1864. Contains a letter from Company "D," the soldiers of Bishop Hill. The letter is written from Rome, Georgia, and is dated June 3, 1864.

William Vipond Pooley: "The Settlement of Illinois from 1830-1850." In the Bulletin of the University of Wisconsin. History Series, Vol. I, Madison, 1902-1908.

Fredrika Bremer: "The Homes of the New World." New York, 1854. In two volumes. Volume two, pp. 67-70, contains some remarks on Eric Janson and the Bishop Hill Colony.